The Mixed Economic Progress of Immigrants

Robert F. Schoeni

Kevin F. McCarthy

Georges Vernez

Supported by
The Ford Foundation and
the James Irvine Foundation

Center for Research on Immigration Policy

RAND

PREFACE

In the midst of large increases in immigration, a relative deterioration in the level of education of immigrants, and slow employment growth, the question of how immigrants perform and progress economically in the United States has once more become salient. This report addresses this question in several unique ways. First, it examines in detail the differences in the rate of economic progress of immigrants from different countries of origin (rather than for all immigrants as a whole) and identifies the reasons for these differences. Second, and for the first time, it assesses whether the economic progress of recent immigrants is slower than that of previous generations of immigrants. Finally, it assesses the economic progress of immigrants in California separately from that of those in the rest of the nation, because, at 26 percent, the share of immigrants in California's labor force is more than three times higher than that in the rest of the United States.

This report is part of a comprehensive study of the effects of immigration on the state of California. It was funded by The Ford Foundation and the James Irvine Foundation. One other report has been published:

> Georges Vernez and Kevin F. McCarthy, *The Costs of Immigration to Taxpayers: Analytical and Policy Issues*, Santa Monica, Calif.: RAND, MR-705-FF/IF, 1996.

Research for the report was conducted in RAND's Center for Research on Immigration Policy.

This report and its companion report should be of interest to policymakers; federal, state, and local officials; advocates; and researchers concerned with gaining a better understanding of the multiple dimensions of immigration and its effects on U.S. society.

CONTENTS

FIGURES

TABLES

The United States has prided itself on being a nation of immigrants, a nation in which peoples from around the world are welcomed and given the opportunity to prosper. With hard work and perseverance, newcomers can better themselves and their families. But is this picture that is so vividly portrayed as the U.S. heritage the reality for today's immigrants? Does the economic well-being of immigrants improve substantially over time, or are most immigrants' wages, which are relatively low when they enter the country, stagnant throughout their working lives?

Today, one out of every four workers in California is born outside of the United States. Only 20 years ago, just one out of every ten workers was foreign-born, marking a significant transformation in the composition of the California workforce. Immigrants arrive in California with a variety of skills, training, and experience. The majority of immigrants are poorly educated and have low English proficiency; however, a substantial proportion is highly skilled, and nearly one-quarter of all working-age immigrants has been educated in the United States. Among all workers in California with a college degree, one in five is an immigrant. In addition, although the single largest group of immigrant workers was born in Mexico, 12 percent was born in Japan, Korea, or China; 9 percent was born in the Philippines; and 8 percent was born in Central America. It is clear that immigrants are a heterogeneous group, which may make the labor market in California more complex than that in other states.

Given the magnitude of immigrant representation in California, to design effective immigration, social, and economic policies, it is crucial to determine how immigrants are progressing in the labor market. Such a determination is the objective of this study. We begin by describing the trends in labor market earnings of immigrant workers and native-born workers in California and in the nation over the past 20 years. The earnings of immigrant workers relative to those of native-born workers have declined substantially. However, there is diversity within the immigrant population, with relative earnings of immigrants originally from certain countries rising significantly. Moreover, at the same time that immigrants have begun to dominate the lowest-skill jobs—85 percent of workers with less than nine years of schooling in California was immigrants in 1990—the largest decline in wages of immigrant workers relative to those of native-born workers has been among the lowest-skill workers. This negative trend is reinforced by the fact that the difference in earnings between the least-skilled workers and the most-skilled workers has grown in the past 15 to 20 years. As a result, a substantial share of the immigrant labor force is earning wages that are significantly lower than native-born workers' wages.

Although the earnings of immigrants may be quite low when they initially enter the United States, do immigrants' earnings increase substantially over time as their English-language skills improve and as they learn how the U.S. labor market functions? And if their wages do grow, do they grow any faster than the wages of native-born workers, reducing the gap that exists at the time of entry? Previous analyses have shown that immigrants experience rapid labor market assimilation, and, after 10 to 15 years, they are earning wages similar to those of native-born workers. This study reassesses these analyses by looking at recent data for California and the nation as a whole, and by investigating the variation in economic progress among immigrants arriving from different countries. We find that Japanese, Korean, and Chinese immigrants enter with wages much lower than those of native-born workers but that their earnings increase rapidly. Within 10 to 15 years, their wages reach parity with those of native-born workers. Europeans enter with wages similar to those of natives and continue to earn comparable wages over their working lives. Mexicans, on the other hand, enter with very low wages and experience a persistent wage gap.

Assuming that education plays an important role in determining labor market success, the study then determines the degree to which differences in completed years of schooling explain the differences in the earnings profiles of the various immigrant groups. For example, if Mexican immigrants complete the same number of years of schooling as native-born workers, are their earnings profiles comparable? The answer is no. Although education is a powerful predictor of earnings and explains some of the disparities in earnings, there is still a substantial difference in earnings profiles between certain immigrant groups and those of native-born workers after differences in education have been adjusted for. However, we do find substantial differences in labor market earnings among those immigrants educated in the United States versus those educated abroad. The former group has a substantially higher number of years of education than those educated abroad, twice as many among Mexicans, which accounts for much of the earnings differences. In addition, the quality of the education received in the United States is higher.

Educational attainment may influence the level of earnings at a particular point in time, and it may also enhance the rate of growth of earnings over an immigrant's lifetime. That is, more-educated immigrants may improve their English-language skills more quickly and learn how the U.S. labor market functions more rapidly than less-educated immigrants. On the other hand, highly educated immigrants may enter the country with knowledge of English already; therefore, the less-educated workers may be able to experience the greatest improvement in English-language skills and, as a result, experience the largest growth in earnings. The findings from the study are mixed; among immigrants arriving from certain countries, the more-educated assimilate more quickly, while for other groups the more-educated assimilate more slowly than the less-educated.

Immigration to California has accelerated rapidly in the past 20 years. Many sectors of the labor market are dominated by immigrants, which may create increased competition for jobs among immigrants. The labor market returns to education have increased; at the same time, immigrants are disproportionately represented in lower-skill jobs. As a result of these trends, immigrants may be finding it more difficult to become assimilated into the labor market.

The final objective of the study is to determine whether there has been a change in the rate of growth in immigrants' relative wages. The evidence suggests that the rate of wage growth (relative to that of

U.S.–born workers) has not accelerated for any immigrant groups. While this is not seen as problematic for some immigrant groups (e.g., Europeans, Canadians, Japanese, Koreans, and Chinese) because they continue to reach parity with native-born workers fairly quickly, for other immigrant groups (e.g., Mexicans and Central Americans), it suggests that the persistent wage gap that they have experienced historically may not diminish in the foreseeable future.

ACKNOWLEDGMENTS

We thank Becky Kilburn and Steve Trejo for their extensive comments, and seminar participants at the University of Southern California, the University of California, Santa Barbara, and RAND.

Chapter One

INTRODUCTION

The United States has prided itself on being a nation of immigrants, a nation in which peoples from around the world are welcomed and given the opportunity to prosper. With hard work and perseverance, newcomers can better themselves and their families. But is this picture that is so vividly portrayed as the U.S. heritage the reality for today's immigrants? Does the economic well-being of immigrants improve substantially over time, or are most immigrants' wages, which are relatively low when they enter the country, stagnant throughout their working lives?

Today, one out of every four workers in California is born outside of the United States. Only 20 years ago, just one out of every ten workers was foreign-born, marking a significant transformation in the composition of the California workforce. Immigrants arrive in California with a variety of skills, training, and experience. The majority of immigrants are poorly educated and have low English proficiency; however, a substantial proportion is highly skilled, and about one-quarter of working-age immigrants is educated in the United States. Among those workers in California with a college degree, one in five is an immigrant. In addition, although the single largest group of immigrant workers was born in Mexico, 12 percent was born in Japan, Korea, or China; 9 percent was born in the Philippines; and 8 percent was born in Central America. It is clear that immigrants are a diverse group, which may cause the labor market in California to be more complex than that in other states.

To design effective immigration, social, and economic policies that take into account the sheer magnitude of the immigrant representation in California, it is crucial to determine how immigrants are progressing in the labor market. Such a determination is the objective of this study. In this chapter, we review past research and present the specific questions addressed in the study.

PAST RESEARCH

A sizable body of literature regarding the integration of immigrants into the U.S. economy has been written in recent years. Perhaps the most influential work to date in this field is Chiswick's (1978) analysis of the effect of foreign birth and length of time in the United States on the earnings of foreign-born white men. Chiswick, using the 1970 Census, found that upon arrival, immigrants earn less than native-born workers with similar characteristics, such as amount of education, years of total labor market experience, and weeks worked during the year. This earnings gap begins to narrow as foreign-born workers acquire post-immigration experience in the U.S. labor market. For example, five years after immigration, foreign-born white men were found to have weekly earnings that were 10 percent lower than the earnings of similar native-born men. However, earnings for the two groups were found to be equal after immigrants had been in the United States approximately 13 years, and after 23 years in the United States, immigrants were found to have earnings that were 6 percent higher than the earnings for similar native-born men. Thus, Chiswick (1978) concludes that "in an analysis of the earnings of immigrants, the number of years since migration is an important variable, and ignoring it would mask important differences between the native and the foreign born and among the foreign born" (p. 918).

Regarding Chiswick's finding that the earnings of immigrants relative to those of native-born workers increase the longer immigrants stay in the United States, a possible explanation may be related to U.S.-specific skills, which native-born workers already possess. For example, substantial benefits may accrue from being able to speak and write English fluently. Since native-born workers are already fluent, only foreign-born workers, some of whom do not initially speak English well, can significantly improve their English-language ability and reap labor market benefits from doing so. As a result, over time we would expect the gap in relative wages of immigrant and native-born workers to narrow. If English-language ability were the primary factor explaining the changing wage gap, then we would expect that the wage gap for immigrants who arrive with good English skills would not diminish as much as that of those who arrive with poor English skills; we examine this hypothesis in Chapter Four by comparing wages for immigrants who arrive from English-speaking countries with those of immigrants who do not. However, there may be other U.S.–specific skills that native-born workers already have and immigrants do not (e.g., information on the local labor market and connections through family and community ties), suggesting that differential wage growth may still exist even for those who arrive with excellent English-language skills.

Chiswick's conclusions stimulated much research about the integration of immigrants into the U.S. labor market (Carliner, 1980; Long, 1980; Borjas, 1982; Stewart and Hyclak, 1984; among others). This body of research, which Borjas (1987) has called "first-generation studies," builds upon Chiswick's research and employs a similar analytic and methodological framework. More recently, questions have been raised regarding the empirical validity of the first-generation studies. New studies have demonstrated that cross-section regressions used in Chiswick's and other first-generation studies confound aging and cohort effects (Borjas 1985, 1987, 1994, 1995; Smith, unpublished). That is, the positive correlation between years since migration and immigrant earnings could be due, for example, to a true assimilation or an aging effect, as posited by Chiswick: The longer immigrants remain in the United States the more they learn about the U.S. labor market and enhance their English ability. However, this relationship in cross-sectional data could exist because immigrants who arrive in the United States at different times in U.S. history have had different skills and abilities, with more-recent immigrants having lower-quality labor-market skills. Therefore, a point-in-time comparison of immigrants who arrived recently with those who arrived several years earlier would find disparities among these groups, even if there were no assimilation effect.[1]

Borjas' (1985) comparison of immigrant cohorts using the 1970 and 1980 Census data suggests that the strong assimilation rates mea-

---

[1]Note, however, that the differences in "quality" as defined by Borjas (1985) must go beyond those differences captured by completed education, because education is controlled for in Chiswick's regressions.

sured in cross-sectional studies such as Chiswick's are partly due to a decline in the "quality," i.e., labor market skills and abilities, of immigrants admitted to the United States since 1950. That is, by holding the number of years since migration constant, Borjas found that earlier immigrant cohorts earn more at every point of their U.S. labor market career than more-recent cohorts. Borjas cites this finding as evidence that the quality of immigrant cohorts has been falling over time, and that cross-sectional analyses of immigrant earnings have overestimated the true growth in immigrant earnings.

However, Greenwood and McDowell (1990) point out that neither the Chiswick nor the Borjas work completely resolves the issues of labor market progress and immigrant "quality." For example, they question the comparability of data collected under different censuses, especially since a larger share of illegal immigrants may have been counted in the 1980 Census than in the 1970 Census. Furthermore, they point out that the consequences of ignoring compositional shifts can be serious. For instance, if the high-income members of a cohort emigrate, then the cohort survivors who initially had low incomes may appear to have made no economic progress when, in actuality, they have increased their earnings.[2] Although data limitations prohibit us from incorporating these dimensions directly into our analyses, we do investigate the extent to which they might confound our results, in the first section in Chapter Four, "Approach."

More-recent work by Borjas (1994, 1995) continues to find that immigrants do not assimilate quickly: "practically all immigrants, regardless of when they arrived in the country, experience the same sluggish relative wage growth" (1994, p. 1679). LaLonde and Topel (1992, p. 85) also find that the wages of immigrant and U.S.–born workers do not necessarily converge over time. However, as they state, "this finding does not imply a lack of assimilation. As we documented above, time in the United States has a strong positive effect on earning capacity, holding constant experience and education." LaLonde and Topel make an important distinction between wage convergence and "assimilation." *Wage convergence* is determined by

---

[2] Recent work by Borjas and Bratsberg (1994) has also begun to address the issue of out-migration.

the sum of the effects of assimilation and the returns to general labor market experience. *Assimilation* is unique to immigrants; however, both immigrants and natives reap the benefits of labor market experience. Although the current evidence suggests that assimilation does occur for some immigrant groups, those groups fail to achieve wage convergence because of differences in the returns to experience between natives and immigrants; we return to this issue in Chapter Four.

Additional recent research has determined that immigrants who arrived as children have higher earnings than those who did not, and that adjusting for age at arrival lowers the estimated rates of assimilation (Friedberg, 1991; Smith, unpublished). Part of the reason for the relationship between wages and age at arrival is that younger immigrants are more likely to attend U.S. schools and, as a result, have perhaps a higher level of schooling and an education that is more highly valued in the U.S. labor market. Examining the latter component, Park (1994) found that immigrants who attended U.S. schools do in fact have higher labor market returns to education than those who did not attend U.S. schools. We provide additional evidence on this issue, examining differences across a more detailed set of country-of-origin groups and utilizing data from the 1970, 1980, and 1990 Censuses.

RESEARCH QUESTIONS

The most recent research findings, which suggest that growth in labor market earnings among immigrants may be slow, raised the following three primary questions:

1. Has the rate of growth in labor market earnings (i.e., the rate of economic progress) varied substantially across immigrants arriving from different countries?

2. What is the role of education in explaining the level and growth in labor market earnings?

3. Has the rate of growth in labor market earnings changed over time? That is, have more-recent immigrants improved their relative economic status at a faster or slower rate than immigrants arriving in earlier periods?

These three questions are the focus of this report. The following paragraphs explain why each was formulated.

With regard to the first question, immigrants from different countries arrive with distinct skills and abilities, and it is quite likely that those skills enable them to advance in the U.S. economy at different rates. Although some previous studies have examined certain country-of-origin (or origin) groups, the groupings have tended to be quite broad.[3] Most notably, the studies that have examined Asians have grouped all Asian immigrants together, even though there are substantial differences in language, education, and skill levels among, for example, Filipinos, Indochinese, and Japanese, Koreans, and Chinese (Borjas, 1994, 1995; LaLonde and Topel, 1992).[4]

Our analyses examine the wage growth among several different origin groups that have not previously been examined and that constitute large and growing shares of the immigrant population: immigrants from Japan, Korea, and China; the Philippines; the Middle East and other Asian countries; Central America; Mexico; Canada and the United Kingdom (UK); and Europe. Our analyses show that there is tremendous disparity in the rates of economic progress among Asians: Some groups achieve rapid growth and reach parity with natives quickly; others do not experience growth in their relative wages even after being in the United States 10 to 20 years.

As to the second question, on the role of education in the rate of growth in labor market earnings, there are substantial differences in completed education among immigrants arriving from different countries. We determine the extent to which differences in labor market earnings among immigrant groups are explained by these disparities.

_____

[3]An exception is Borjas (1987), who separately examined 41 countries using data from 1970 and 1980. However, unlike our analyses, Borjas' analysis does not examine data from 1990; examines only the nation as a whole, not California in particular; and does not investigate the differential rate of assimilation across education groups.

[4]Borjas (1985, footnote 11), Borjas (1994, p. 1683), and Borjas (1995, p. 27) do mention that aggregating Asians from different countries may be problematic, but we are aware of no study that has disaggregated these groups using the 1990 Census. Kossoudji (1988) reduces the aggregation problem by grouping together only East Asians, but there is still likely to be substantial variation among these immigrants. Note that Kossoudji's sample had only 548 East Asians, so disaggregation was probably not feasible.

Furthermore, it is quite likely that the rate of economic progress is different between more- and less-educated immigrants. The process of assimilation includes learning a new language and learning how the U.S. labor market functions. It is possible that assimilation may be more rapid for those with more education, because they have the ability and skills to acquire such information more quickly. However, highly educated immigrants are more likely than less-educated immigrants to enter the country with knowledge of English; therefore, the less-educated have the opportunity to reap the largest benefits from learning the language.[5] Therefore, we test whether the rate of labor market assimilation differs among immigrants having different education levels.

As part of answering question 2, we also investigate the variation in labor market performance between those immigrants who did attend U.S. schools and those who did not. Nationally, 27 percent of prime-aged (25–60-year-old) immigrant males attended schools in the United States. As we demonstrate, the structure and profile of wages of these immigrants are distinct from those of immigrants who received all their schooling abroad. Moreover, the earnings difference between those educated and those not educated in the United States varies among immigrants arriving from different countries.

The labor market returns to education have changed substantially in the United States over the past 20 years: The gap between more- and less-skilled workers has become larger. Because immigrant groups are predominantly low-skilled, the changing structure of wages (i.e., "prices" of skills) may have harmed immigrants substantially (LaLonde and Topel, 1992). We investigate this issue. In addition, we determine whether the changes in the earnings differentials across education groups that have been experienced among native-born workers in the past 20 years also have been experienced among immigrants from various countries.

The third primary question, whether the rate of growth in labor market earnings has changed over time, stems from the scale of immi-

---

[5]Note that Baker and Benjamin (1994, p. 393) posit that one reason assimilation may have changed over time in Canada is that more-recent immigrant workers have been less skilled (relative to native-born workers) than earlier immigrants. However, they do not directly test whether assimilation does in fact vary by skill level.

gration. Given the large increase in that scale, it is quite possible that immigrants are finding it more difficult to improve their economic position because they are competing with a larger number of similarly skilled immigrants in the labor market. However, the existence of a large group of fellow immigrants from the same country or region may serve as an important resource and enhance labor market achievement. Baker and Benjamin (1994) have addressed this issue for Canada, examining the change in the rate of economic progress between 1971 and 1981 and between 1981 and 1986. Borjas (1995) provides recent evidence on the change of economic progress between the 1970s and 1980s for the United States, although he does not examine the variation across countries of origin in the detail that we do.

UNIQUE CONTRIBUTIONS

Whereas several previous studies have addressed the economic progress of immigrants, this study is unique in combining several dimensions, some of which have been examined individually by other studies: First, it is the only study that examines immigrants separately by country of origin, using the 1970, 1980, and 1990 Censuses simultaneously.[6] Second, the empirical specifications of experience, education, and assimilation are less restrictive than the specifications employed in prior work. Third, the study examines whether assimilation varies by the education level of the immigrants. Fourth, the study examines in more detail the characteristics of immigrants arriving from different countries, especially those of immigrants from Asia. Previous studies have grouped many immigrants arriving from different countries and having distinct labor market processes.[7] Fifth, the study examines differences in wage profiles by

---

[6]A recent article by Borjas (1995) uses the three censuses, but the only specific country of origin that he examines is Mexico, and he does not allow assimilation to vary by education level. However, Borjas (1987) disaggregates immigrants by country of origin but does not examine the 1990 Census or allow the rate of assimilation to vary by education.

[7]An exception is Borjas (1987), although it appears that he used a more restrictive specification. For example, it appears that the effects of age and education are not allowed to vary between immigrant and native-born workers, the returns to education are not allowed to vary by age, and age is specified as a quadratic. Yuengart (1994) finds that the estimates of wages of immigrant workers relative to those of native-born

whether immigrants were educated in the United States, including differences in returns to schooling and changes in immigrant "quality" between those who did and did not attend U.S. schools.[8] Sixth, it provides evidence of whether the wage growth has changed between the 1970s and the 1980s; Baker and Benjamin (1994) provide similar evidence for Canada, and Borjas (1994) presents evidence for the United States, but not for immigrants arriving from as detailed a set of origin groups. Finally, it examines California separately, in addition to the United States as a whole.[9]

ORGANIZATION OF THIS REPORT

The report proceeds as follows. We discuss data and variables analyzed and define the country groupings in Chapter Two. Then, before discussing the analyses of each of the three questions, we present, in Chapter Three, background information on immigrants in California and the United States as a whole, including estimates of the share of workers who are immigrants and the trend in their employment and earnings relative to native workers' earnings over the past 20 years. We address the three research questions in Chapter Four, and in Chapter Five we summarize the findings. Throughout the study, we emphasize the findings for California because of the large share of immigrants in its workforce; however, for the methodological reason discussed in Chapter Three and for comparison, we also conducted all analyses for the United States (also referred to as *the nation*) as a whole.

---

workers are sensitive to the specification of age as a quartic instead of a quadratic, and that the quartic, which is the specification that we use, is preferable.

[8]Park (1994) examines the returns to schooling, i.e., increases in earnings associated with increases in schooling, for those who did and did not attend more than six years of schooling outside the United States, using the 1980 and 1990 Censuses; however, the emphasis of his study is not immigrant labor market performance per se, and, except for Mexicans, he examines only broad groups of immigrants arriving from different countries. Friedberg (1991) examines the role of age at migration, which is very closely related to the role of attendance at U.S. schools, as discussed in Chapter Four.

[9]Two other recent studies have been done on assimilation of immigrants across different regions of the nation. Garvey (1995) examines assimilation of immigrants in New Jersey; the study by Reimers (1995) analyzes Mexican immigrants in California and Texas.

Chapter Two

DATA AND COUNTRY-OF-ORIGIN GROUPINGS

The analyses are based on the 1970, 1980, and 1990 Public Use Micro Samples of the U.S. Census. In all descriptive analyses, the sample weights are used to produce unbiased population estimates.[1] The key variables examined include country of birth, year arrived in the United States (or arrival year), employment status, earnings, and education. An *immigrant* is defined as someone who was born in a foreign country; those who were born abroad of American parents (e.g., individuals whose parents were in the U.S. military and stationed abroad at the time the person was born) are considered native-born U.S. citizens.

Men and women have distinct labor market processes, and it is important to examine both. In this report, however, we examine only men. Analyses of women will be reported in a separate study. For all analyses, immigrants from certain countries are grouped together on the basis of several criteria:

- First, each origin group must constitute a significant share of the immigrant population.

- Second, most groupings include countries that are geographically close to each other.

- Third, and most important, the individuals from the countries that are grouped together must have common backgrounds and

---

[1]Note that the 1970 and 1980 Censuses are self-weighting. Sample weights are not used in the regression analyses.

experiences (e.g., language) that would lead them to have similar experiences in the U.S. labor market.

These criteria resulted in the nine country groupings listed in Table 2.1; groups are ranked in order of the share they represented among the immigrant population in California in 1990. Although most groups are narrowly defined, some groups, especially groups 6 and 7, are heterogeneous. As a result, we do not place as much emphasis on the results for those countries.

Employment status is based on the individual's reported activity in the week prior to the census. For most analyses, the *earnings* are weekly wages, which include self-employment and wage and salary income. Those with negative earnings from a loss in business income were excluded. For the 1970 Census, the number of weeks worked was reported in six categories, or brackets: 13 or fewer, 14–26, 27–39, 40–47, 48–49, and 50–52. To calculate weekly earnings in 1970, we used the median of each of the intra-bracket distributions for weeks worked reported in 1980. These values are, respectively, 7.818, 21.044, 32.926. 42.310, 48.200, and 51.769 weeks. Wages are expressed in 1990 dollars, using the Consumer Price Index for urban consumers.

Table 2.1

Percentage of Immigrant Men in the Labor Force Who Are from Each Country-of-Origin Group, in California and the Nation (1990)

Country-of-Origin Group	California	Nation
1. Mexico	37.4	21.5
2. Japan, Korea, and China	12.0	10.4
3. Central America	8.7	5.8
4. Philippines	8.5	5.3
5. Europe	8.2	17.0
6. Middle East and all other Asian countries not listed in the table	7.6	8.2
7. Africa, Caribbean, South America, and Oceania	6.7	20.1
8. Indochina and Vietnam	5.9	4.0
9. United Kingdom (UK) and Canada	5.0	7.6
TOTAL	100.0	100.0

NOTE: Final totals have been rounded off.

For most analyses, we grouped workers into various education categories, paralleling the census categories. For 1970 and 1980, education is reported in completed years of schooling and the classification into the categories is straightforward. The question in the census on educational attainment changed in 1990 by (among other things) asking for explicit degrees beyond high school, as opposed to years of completed education. In constructing the education categories with the 1990 data, we included individuals with a General Education Degree with those having 12 years of schooling; we coded individuals with some college or an associate's degree as having 13–15 years of schooling; we coded individuals with a bachelor's degree as having 16 years of schooling; and we coded individuals with advanced degrees as having 17 or more years of schooling. For analyses in which we distinguish those with more than 16 years of schooling, we include those with an advanced degree in this highest category.

Chapter Three

NATIVE-BORN AND IMMIGRANT WORKERS:
20 YEARS OF CHANGE

Before turning to the central analyses of growth in labor market earnings in Chapter Four, we present background information regarding the immigrant and native-born workforces in California and the nation, as follows. We first document the change in the size and education composition of the immigrant workforce relative to those of the native-born workforce, along with the change in the country-of-origin mix among immigrants. We then examine the changes in labor-force participation and unemployment rates among native-born workers and immigrant workers from different countries. Finally, we describe changes in cross-sectional earnings differences among native-born and immigrant workers and analyze the role of education in these cross-sectional disparities.

SIZE AND COMPOSITION OF MALE LABOR FORCE

The California (male) labor force has undergone a tremendous transformation in the past 20 years (Table 3.1). The approximately 452,000 immigrant male workers in California in 1960 represented 10 percent of the male workforce. The share of immigrants remained constant at about 10 percent over the subsequent ten years. However, the immigrant population doubled during the 1970s, leading to a rise to 17 percent in the share of the California workforce who were immigrants in 1980. The number of male immigrants doubled again in the 1980s; as a result, one out of every four male workers in California in 1990 was an immigrant.

Immigrant representation in the nation as a whole is much lower than that in just California. Nationally in 1960, 6 percent of the male

Table 3.1

Number of Male Immigrant Workers and Their Share of the Male Workforce, in California and the Nation (1960–1990)

	California			Nation		
Census	Native-Born	Immigrants	Percentage Who Are Immigrants	Native-Born	Immigrants	Percentage Who Are Immigrants
1960	3,943,000	452,000	10.3	42,353,000	2,651,000	5.9
1970	4,788,000	531,000	10.0	46,878,000	2,383,000	4.8
1980	5,583,000	1,139,000	16.9	55,343,000	3,933,000	6.6
1990	6,299,000	2,320,175	26.9	59,779,000	6,576,000	9.9

workforce was immigrants. Although immigrant representation grew in the national workforce during the 1970s and 1980s, it grew faster in California. The immigrant share increased nationally from 5 percent in 1970 to 10 percent in 1990—a 100-percent increase. In California, the change during the same period, from 10 to 27 percent, represents a 169-percent increase. Therefore, although immigrants have historically formed a larger share of the California labor force than of the national labor force, this disparity has increased substantially in the past two decades.

Immigrants from different countries arrive with different education, skills, and English-language abilities; as a result, their successes in the labor market also differ. Historically, relative to the nation as a whole, a greater share of California's immigrants has arrived from Mexico; in 1970, an immigrant in California was five times more likely to be from Mexico than was an immigrant in the United States as a whole (Table 3.2). European immigrants have constituted a much larger share of the immigrant workforce in the nation than in California. These patterns continue to hold today: 40 percent of immigrant workers in California have arrived from Mexico. In both California and the nation, the share of immigrants who are Europeans has declined dramatically, representing just 7 percent of immigrant workers in California and 20 percent in the nation in 1990. At the same time, immigration from Asia—especially from Japan, Korea, and China, the Philippines, and Indochina—has risen significantly, composing almost 25 percent of the immigrant labor force in California and over 15 percent in the nation.

Table 3.2

Percentage of Male Immigrant Workers in Each Origin Group, in California and the Nation (1970–1990)

	Percentage					
	California			United States		
Orgin Group	1970	1980	1990	1970	1980	1990
Mexico	24.3	37.8	39.9	5.1	9.6	15.6
Japan, Korea, China	7.5	9.9	10.7	3.3	6.7	8.5
Central America	2.8	5.3	9.7	1.4	2.7	5.2
Philippines	5.6	8.4	8.9	1.9	3.9	4.2
Europe	26.9	14.2	7.4	46.8	32.1	19.5
Middle East, Other Asia	4.5	5.5	6.8	3.5	6.5	8.5
Africa, Caribbean, South America, Oceania	8.3	7.2	6.5	17.1	24.4	27.4
Indochina, Vietnam	0.1	1.8	4.8	0.1	1.6	3.2
UK, Canada	19.4	9.3	4.9	20.7	11.8	7.8

Labor market success depends largely on education, and the share of the least-educated workers who are immigrants has skyrocketed. In 1990 in California, 85 percent of all male workers with less than nine years of schooling was immigrants, up from 26 percent in 1970 (Table 3.3). For the nation as a whole, 39 percent of men with less than nine years of schooling was immigrants compared with 9 percent in 1970. Increases in immigration have kept the number of low-skill workers in California higher than in the nation as a whole. In 1970, workers in the United States were 50 percent (=(21.4 – 13.9)/13.9) more likely to be among the lowest-skilled group than were workers in California. By 1990, just the opposite was the case: California workers were 50 percent more likely to be among the least educated (=(8.6 – 5.5)/5.5).

Among those with 12 years of schooling in California, the share of workers who were immigrants tripled between 1970 and 1990. However, growth in immigrant representation has also increased significantly for the highest educated: The share of immigrants among those with 16 or more years of schooling more than doubled between 1970 and 1990, rising from 8 to 20 percent.

Table 3.3

**Percentage of Workers Who Are Immigrants, by Education Level,
in California and the Nation (1970–1990)**

Years of Schooling	Percentage of All Workers with Given Years of Schooling			Percentage of Immigrant Workers Among Those with Given Years of Schooling		
	1970	1980	1990	1970	1980	1990
In California						
0–8	13.9	9.2	8.6	25.9	58.9	85.4
9–11	16.6	9.6	6.1	8.1	17.6	37.3
12	30.7	27.7	23.2	7.2	11.5	21.9
13–15	19.3	25.6	32.3	7.9	11.0	16.3
16 or more	19.5	27.8	29.8	7.9	13.8	19.5
All workers				10.0	16.9	26.9
In the United States						
0–8	21.4	11.0	5.5	8.8	16.3	39.1
9–11	19.3	12.8	8.2	3.7	5.6	9.8
12	31.5	34.0	31.5	3.6	4.6	6.9
13–15	11.9	18.4	27.7	5.1	5.9	7.2
16 or more	15.7	23.6	27.0	3.9	7.6	9.9
All workers				4.8	6.6	9.9

In sum, although immigrants dominate the lowest-skilled jobs in California, they now also represent a substantial share of the highly skilled workforce in the state.

EMPLOYMENT STATUS

Participation in the labor force, i.e., the share of people who are either working or are looking for work, is similar for both native-born and immigrant men in California. In 1990, the participation rate was 87 percent for native-born men and 89 percent for immigrant men (Table 3.4). Among prime-aged males, labor force participation of both natives and immigrants has decreased slightly over the past 20 years, which is consistent with previous studies (e.g., Parsons, 1980). In 1970, the labor force participation rate was 91 percent for both natives and immigrants. The levels and trends in California parallel those for the nation.

Table 3.4

Employment Status of Native-Born and Immigrant Men 25–64 Years Old, in California and the Nation (1970–1990)

	Percentage					
	1970		1980		1990	
Employment Status	Native-Born Men	Immigrant Men	Native-Born Men	Immigrant Men	Native-Born Men	Immigrant Men
In California						
In the labor force	91	91	88	89	87	89
Unemployed	4.2	4.4	4.7	5.6	4.6	6.8
In the United States						
In the labor force	91	91	88	89	87	90
Unemployed	2.7	3.2	4.8	5.3	4.8	6.1

NOTE: Based on reported employment status during the week prior to the census.

However, for immigrants, unemployment rates are higher—a disadvantage that has increased in both California and the United States as a whole. In 1990 in California, 6.8 percent of all immigrant men who were in the labor force were unemployed, whereas 4.6 percent of native men were unemployed. Furthermore, in 1990, the share of unemployed was slightly higher in California than in the nation, but the unemployment rate among natives was lower for those living in California. As is shown below, this disparity is a result of the disproportionate concentration of Mexicans in California, a group that has a relatively high unemployment rate.

Although the differences in labor force participation between native-born men and immigrant men are not large in the aggregate, the disparities among immigrants from different countries are substantial. The most significant difference in workforce participation is for prime-aged males from Indochina and Vietnam (Table 3.5), 30 percent of whom did not work in 1990—a share two to three times greater than that of other immigrants who did not work. And Indochinese and Vietnamese immigrants in California are 30 percent less likely to work than those who live anywhere in the United States. Part of this difference is explained by the fact that a disproportionate percentage of the Hmong relative to other Indochinese groups are located in California and have lower participation rates.[1]

Among those Indochinese and Vietnamese who do participate in the labor force, a higher share is unemployed: 9.3 percent in California in 1990; the next highest rate, 8.5 percent, was for Mexicans and Central Americans. Many immigrant groups had rates closer to 5.0 percent—close to the unemployment rate of 4.6 percent for native-born men.

Unemployment among some immigrant groups—Japan, Korea, and China, the Philippines, and the United Kingdom and Canada—was less prevalent than among native-born workers in 1990, both in California and the nation. In California, these origin groups represented 25 percent of all immigrants in 1990.

EARNINGS

The overall difference in earnings between immigrant and native-born men in California increased over the 20-year period shown in Table 3.6. Among men in California in 1970, immigrants made, on average, 84 percent of the earnings of natives.[2] The relative earnings of immigrants decreased slightly to 80 percent in 1980, and this change was followed by a further decline in the 1980s, with relative earnings of just 72 percent by 1990.

In sum, immigrants as a group have traditionally earned significantly less than natives in California, and this gap increased between 1970 and 1990.

---

[1]Specifically, 52 percent of Hmong, 46 percent of Cambodians, and 39 percent of Laotians in the United States reside in California. Of all the Vietnamese in the United States, 45 percent reside in California.

[2]Throughout the study, we compare each immigrant group with one reference group of workers: natives as a whole. Because native-born workers of various races, ethnicities, and national heritages earn different wages, comparison of immigrants' earnings with the earnings of native-born workers of similar race, ethnicity, or heritage would lead to different results, as other studies have shown. However, if the public is concerned about immigrants' earnings because of the implications for tax revenue and public-service use, then a common comparison group is preferable.

Table 3.5

Employment Status of 25–64-Year-Old Men by Country of Origin, in California and the Nation (1970–1990)

| | Percentage | | | | | |
| | 1970 | | 1980 | | 1990 | |
Country of Origin	In the Labor Force	Unemployment Rate	In the Labor Force	Unemployment Rate	In the Labor Force	Unemployment Rate
	In California					
Mexico	90	6.0	92	8.0	91	8.5
Japan, Korea, China	87	4.3	88	2.8	88	3.4
Central America	91	7.7	92	7.1	92	8.5
Philippines	91	4.4	93	3.4	94	4.2
Europe	92	3.2	90	3.6	87	4.8
Middle East, Other Asia	89	2.6	83	5.3	88	5.4
Africa, Caribbean, South America, Oceania	93	6.2	89	4.2	90	5.4
Indochina, Vietnam	—[a]	—[a]	67	9.7	70	9.3
UK, Canada	93	3.4	89	2.8	91	3.4
Born U.S. Citizen	91	4.2	88	4.7	87	4.6

Table 3.5—continued

Country of Origin	Percentage					
	1970		1980		1990	
	In the Labor Force	Unemployment Rate	In the Labor Force	Unemployment Rate	In the Labor Force	Unemployment Rate
	In the United States					
Mexico	89	4.7	92	8.0	91	8.3
Japan, Korea, China	86	2.4	88	2.7	87	3.1
Central America	93	3.6	91	6.5	92	7.1
Philippines	92	2.7	94	3.2	93	3.9
Europe	92	3.0	91	4.7	88	5.3
Middle East, Other Asia	89	2.6	86	4.5	90	4.7
Africa, Caribbean, South America, Oceania	93	3.5	90	5.3	89	6.6
Indochina, Vietnam	—a	—a	75	9.2	77	7.0
UK, Canada	92	3.4	89	3.6	90	3.6
Born U.S. Citizen	91	2.7	88	4.8	87	4.9

aToo few observations.

Table 3.6

Earnings of Immigrant Workers Relative to Those of Native-Born Workers, 25–64-Year-Old Men in California and the Nation (1970–1990)[a]

| Earnings Percentile | Percentage | | | | | |
| | California | | | United States | | |
	1970	1980	1990	1970	1980	1990
Mean	84	80	72	99	93	89
5th (lowest)	79	77	74	104	82	84
10th	75	75	68	94	79	63
25th	75	69	60	97	79	68
50th	80	70	61	94	83	72
75th	86	80	70	98	89	82
90th	87	81	73	99	91	87
95th (highest)	83	82	71	100	96	88

[a]For example, the ratio of the 75th percentile in the immigrant earnings distribution to the 75th percentile in the native-born earnings distribution in California in 1970 was 0.86.

In California in 1990, the earnings of immigrant men were lower than those of native-born men for the United States as a whole—by 17 percentage points. This difference is due primarily to the higher wages earned by natives in California than by natives in the nation; the ratio of U.S. immigrant to California immigrant earnings is 0.95; the U.S./California ratio for native-born workers is 0.84. However, the trend toward immigrants' wages being lower than natives' wages is reflected in the nation as well. Immigrants' wages, which were comparable to natives' for the nation, had a mean fall to 89 percent in 1990.

For the nation, the largest reduction in relative wages of men has been among the lowest-paid workers. The earnings of immigrants in the lowest 10th percentile of the immigrant earnings distribution relative to the earnings of native-born workers in the 10th percentile of the native-born worker earnings distribution declined from 94 percent to 63 percent between 1970 and 1990 (Table 3.6). For those in the 90th percentile, this difference was 99 percent in 1970 and 87 percent in 1990. Therefore, immigrants at the lowest end of the wage distribution have experienced the most-significant declines in relative wages.

While there is a gap between the earnings of natives and immigrants as a whole, we would expect some immigrants to do better than natives, because those immigrants are highly educated and skilled. This is, in fact, the case (Table 3.7). On average, immigrants from the United Kingdom and Canada do better than natives, and their relative position has increased over the two study decades. Similarly, those from Europe and the Middle East and other Asian countries have earnings that are comparable to natives'; this comparability has held over time.

In 1970 in California, the Japanese, Koreans, and Chinese earned about 25 percent less than natives. But in 20 years, this gap had declined significantly, and these groups earned virtually the same as natives, on average, in 1990. Filipinos also experienced improvements in their relative wages, from 64 percent in 1970 to 74 percent

Table 3.7

Earnings of Immigrant Workers Relative to Those of Native-Born Workers by Country of Origin, 25–64-Year-Old Men in California and the Nation (1970–1990)

| | Percentage | | | | | |
| | California | | | United States | | |
Country of Origin	1970	1980	1990	1970	1980	1990
Mexico	60	58	50	66	65	56
Japan, Korea, China	72	86	98	88	99	110
Central America	74	60	49	79	72	62
Philippines	64	74	74	76	94	93
Europe	103	110	111	110	107	115
Middle East, Other Asia	92	98	98	107	112	120
Africa, Caribbean, South America, Oceania	77	86	92	80	85	86
Indochina, Vietnam	—	59	67	—	66	73
UK, Canada	106	112	121	113	120	130
All Immigrants	84	80	72	99	93	89

NOTE: Appendix Table A.3 reports the relative median earnings. The patterns are, in general, similar. Notable exceptions are for Filipino and Japanese, Korean, and Chinese immigrants. The relative median earnings for Japanese, Korean, and Chinese men in 1990 in California were 88 percent; the relative mean earnings were 98 percent. For Filipino men in the United States in 1990, the relative median earnings were 83 percent; the relative mean earnings were 93 percent. The relative median (73 percent) and mean (74 percent) earnings among Filipino men in California in 1990, however, are similar.

in 1990. At the same time, immigrants from Central America and Mexico experienced substantial reductions in relative wages, from about 25 to 40 percent less than natives in 1970 to 50 percent less in 1990.

The earnings for each immigrant group relative to natives' earnings are lower if the groups are located in California. The difference is most dramatic for those from the Philippines; Japan, Korea, and China; the Middle East and other Asian countries; and Central America. For example, in California in 1990, Filipino men earned 74 percent of the wages of native Californian men, whereas for the United States as a whole, Filipino men earned 93 percent of the wages of native men. These differences are explained primarily by the fact that natve-born men earn higher wages in California.

EDUCATION AND EARNINGS

The differences in relative earnings between immigrant and native-born workers are due in part to disparities in educational attainment. Table 3.8 reports the earnings of immigrant male workers relative to those of native-born workers by completed education, in California and the nation. For California, the earnings gap is reduced by as much as 15 to 20 percentage points when all workers' earnings are viewed in educational groups. For example, the gap for immigrants as a whole was 28 percent in California in 1990 (Table 3.7), but it was only 10 to 20 percent within most education groups.

The disparity in earnings between natives and immigrants also varies substantially across educational levels. In California in 1970, the earnings gap was the greatest for the least educated and the most educated, and smallest for the middle educated workers (i.e., those with 10–15 years of schooling). This was not the case for the United States as a whole, however; instead, the gap was the greatest among the most educated.

The amount of change in the wage gap over time has differed across education levels. While the relative earnings for the most educated have stayed fairly constant in both California and the nation, the gap for those with 12 or fewer years of schooling has grown substantially. Among high school graduates in California in 1970, the relative earnings of immigrant men were 96 percent; by 1990 they were just

Table 3.8

Mean Earnings of Immigrant Workers Relative to Those of Native-Born Workers by Education Level, 25–64-Year-Old Men in California and the Nation (1970–1990)

| Years of Schooling | Percentage | | | | | |
| | California | | | United States | | |
	1970	1980	1990	1970	1980	1990
0–4	88	73	72	120	92	93
5–8	88	71	70	112	93	89
9	103	75	69	109	98	94
10	93	87	83	106	94	100
11	92	94	89	109	99	96
12	96	88	82	102	93	95
13–15	90	93	88	95	94	95
16	80	83	84	89	90	90
17 or more	87	90	82	91	102	91
All Workers	84	80	72	99	94	89

NOTE: A finer categorization of education across all years is not available because the 1990 Census grouped all individuals with 0–4 years and all individuals with 5–8 years of schooling into two separate categories. In addition, incompatible classifications between the 1990 Census and earlier censuses limit the ability to consistently disaggregate in any greater detail those with high levels of education.

82 percent. And for the least educated (i.e., those with less than five years of schooling), relative earnings fell from 88 percent in 1970 to 72 percent in 1990. Similarly, for the least educated nationwide, the relative wages dropped from 120 percent to 93 percent.

Part of this decline is due to changes in the age distribution of less-educated workers. The upgrading in U.S. education since 1970 means that native workers who had 0–4 years of schooling in 1990 were likely to be older workers. On the other hand, many new, young immigrants are arriving with 0–4 years of schooling. As a result, the age difference between poorly educated immigrant workers and native-born workers has increased. And because wages increase with age, there is an increasing disparity between the wages of poorly educated immigrants and those of natives.

To clarify this issue, we estimated the extent to which the differences in earnings between immigrant and native-born workers could be explained by differentials in education and age. The results are shown for California in Figure 3.1 for the 1970, 1980, and 1990

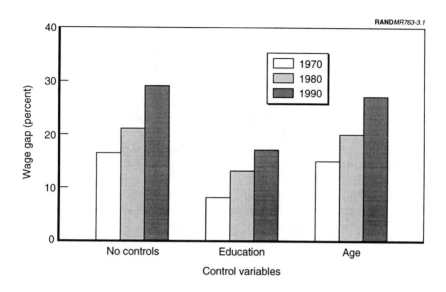

Figure 3.1—Wage Gap Between Immigrant and Native-Born Workers in
California, With and Without Controls (1970–1990)

Census years. We report the gross difference in wages, the difference
after adjusting for education, and the difference after adjusting for
age.[3]

Adjusting for age reduces the difference, slightly. However, adjusting
for differences in education between immigrants and natives reduces
the wage gap by almost one-half in each year. In 1970, the difference
drops from 16 to 9 percent, and in 1990 it declines from 29 to 17 percent after education is adjusted for.[4]

---

[3]Specifically, the controls for education are indicator variables representing 0–4 years,
5–8 years, 9, 10, 11, and 12 years, 13–15 years, 16 years, and 17 or more years. Age is
specified as a quadratic.

[4]For education groups that are more broadly defined (e.g., 0–4, 5–8 and more than 17
years), some of the disparity in earnings and perhaps some of the increase in the disparity may be due to differential distribution in education between immigrants and
natives within the broad category.

The differences between native workers and immigrant workers from various countries are also explained largely by differences in educational attainment.[5] For example, one-half of the wage gap experienced by Mexicans in 1990 can be explained by differences in completed education, which also explain one-third of the wage gap for those from Central America (Figure 3.2). Controlling for educational differences *increases* the wage gap for those from Japan, Korea, and China, and the Middle East and other Asian countries in 1990, because the educational level of these immigrant groups is higher than the educational level of natives, on average.

The educational differences also explain the majority of the disparities across immigrant groups. In 1990, for example, after education is controlled for, immigrants from all countries except Europe, and

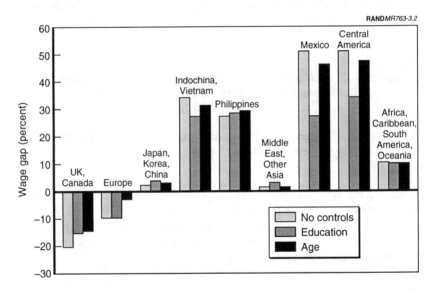

Figure 3.2—Wage Gap Between Immigrant and Native-Born Workers in California by Country of Origin, With and Without Controls (1990)

---

[5]For the analyses of differences across origin groups, the same wage equations are estimated, but instead of a single indicator for whether the worker is an immigrant, there are separate indicators for whether the worker was born in the given country, and native-born workers are the reference category.

the UK and Canada have earnings that are within 20 percentage points of each other. This finding is significant, especially among Mexicans and Central Americans, because there is about a 50-percent unadjusted difference between the wages of these immigrants and those of immigrants from Japan, Korea, and China, and the Middle East and other Asian countries. Age differences, on the other hand, do not explain a large share of the disparities between natives and immigrants, except perhaps for immigrants from Europe and the UK and Canada.

Chapter Four

EARNINGS OF IMMIGRANTS OVER THEIR LIFETIME

The analyses in Chapter Three have shown that there are substantial differences in earnings between immigrant and native-born workers and that this gap has increased over time for immigrants as a whole. However, these analyses have not addressed the central question: How do immigrants' earnings change over their lifetimes? We now focus on this issue by addressing the three primary questions identified in Chapter One. We first describe the approach taken in the analyses. We then estimate the economic progress for each immigrant country-of-origin group (i.e., Question 1). In subsequent sections, we examine the role of education in explaining economic progress (i.e., Question 2) and whether the rate of economic progress has changed (i.e., Question 3).

APPROACH

Ideally, to determine the degree to which immigrants' earnings change following their entry into the United States, we would have a longitudinal data set of periodic interviews with the same immigrants (and natives) over a certain number of years. With this information, earnings and employment outcomes could be traced over an individual immigrant's working life and compared with the pattern for natives. However, such data do not currently exist.[1] Therefore, we employ the "cohort method," which is similar to others (Baker and Benjamin, 1994; Borjas, 1985, 1993, 1995; Friedberg, 1991;

---

[1]Chiswick (1986) examines the National Longitudinal Survey, which follows respondents over time; however, that survey interviewed only 98 immigrants.

LaLonde and Topel, 1992; Smith, unpublished)—using the information on age and date of entry into the United States contained in the 1970, 1980, and 1990 Censuses—to investigate changes in immigrants' labor market outcomes. We follow a given age-specific immigration-year entry group from 1970 to 1980 to 1990. For example, we can compare the earnings reported in the 1970 Census of 25–34-year-olds who immigrated between 1965 and 1969 with those who were 35–44 years old in the 1980 Census and who also reported that they immigrated between 1965 and 1969. This same cohort can then be followed through the 1980s by examining the earnings of 45–54-year-olds as reported in the 1990 Census. The earnings of these immigrants can be compared with the earnings of native-born workers of comparable age to determine whether there is any improvement in the relative earnings of immigrants.

Although the cohort approach is the best technique for determining the extent of wage growth from available data, it has limitations, each of which concerns changes over time in the population covered by the census. For example, some immigrants (and natives) leave the country between censuses. Ahmed and Robinson (1994) estimated that 11.3 percent of the 1980 foreign-born population in the United States emigrated by 1990; therefore, the underlying immigrant population has changed. If the immigrants who leave the country are the ones who are having a difficult time adapting to the labor market, then the estimates from the cohort analysis would overstate the degree of economic progress. In fact, Borjas (1989) found that, for immigrant scientists and engineers, emigration was more likely among those who did less well in the U.S. labor market. On the other hand, if the most successful emigrated, then the estimates of economic progress would be understated.

To assess the severity of this limitation, we examined completed education of those who stayed and those who left by tracking immigrant cohorts across censuses. Although adult immigrants (and natives) may upgrade their education between censuses, upgrading is not likely among older adults. We examined immigrants and natives separately by age.[2] Our analyses are discussed in more detail in the Appendix; here, we summarize our findings.

Although some immigrants leave between censuses, it is not clear that there are systematic differences in emigration by education. The education distribution for a given arrival year–age cohort does appear to be upgraded between censuses, but not dramatically. And the upgrading in education that exists among immigrants is similar in magnitude to the upgrading taking place among natives. This evidence suggests that differential emigration by education may not be substantial and, as a result, the estimates of wage growth are unlikely to be biased significantly. However, it may still be true that the least- (or most-) successful immigrants *within* education groups emigrate; if so, the cohort analysis would overstate (or understate) true wage growth.

In addition to the complications discussed above, which arise for analyses of the United States as a whole, the analyses of California are hampered by the fact that, between census years, some immigrants (and natives) move between states within the United States, which induces changes in the arrival year–age cohorts within California. To gauge the magnitude of this problem, we examined the change in the education distribution for natives and immigrants in California, as we did for the nation. In general, we found that the changes in the education distribution among natives and immigrants are similar. Moreover, by comparing the estimates of economic progress for the nation and for California, we can, to some degree, validate the findings for California.

In sum, although we do not suspect that selective emigration is significantly biasing our estimates of earnings growth, the available supporting evidence is only suggestive, not definitive. Until longi-

---

[2]Of course, emigration may be different for younger than for older immigrants. If so, the results for older immigrants cannot be generalized to individuals of all ages. Also, the reported education of individuals may increase over time, even though their true education has not increased because of rising education norms. Our comparison of changes between immigrants relative to those for natives will overcome this problem if the change in norms has been similar for natives and immigrants.

tudinal data of immigrants become available, it will be difficult to gauge the extent of the bias introduced by nonrandom emigration.

LIFETIME ECONOMIC PROGRESS

We begin our analysis by presenting the relative average earnings of immigrants and natives over time, using the cohort method in its simplest form. These analyses allow us to determine the rate of economic progress achieved by the various immigrant groups. To determine the role of education, and in order to separate out the effects of experience and assimilation, we then conduct multivariate analyses, which are an extension of the cohort method; the multivariate analyses are described more fully in the Appendix.

Tracking Arrival Cohorts

Tables 4.1 and 4.2 display the cohort analysis for men who were 25–34 years old in 1970 for the three largest immigrant groups in California and the United States—Mexicans, Europeans, and Japanese, Koreans, and Chinese. In California, these three groups accounted for 38 percent, 12 percent, and 10 percent of prime-aged immigrants (i.e., 25–60-year-olds), respectively, enumerated in the 1970, 1980, and 1990 Censuses combined. These three groups also represent the extremes in economic progress: Japanese, Koreans, and Chinese immigrants experienced the highest rate of economic progress while Mexicans have had the lowest rate among all groups considered.

Immigrants' real earnings increase with the length of time spent in the United States (Table 4.2). For example, among Mexicans, immigrants who arrived between 1965 and 1969 and who were 25–34 years old in 1970 had median weekly wages of $320 in 1970 in California, $405 ten years later, and by 1990, when they were 45 to 55 years old, $391 (which is actually a slight decline in real wages). The growth in earnings among Europeans was greater for the same arrival year: Europeans entering between 1965 and 1969 and who were 25–34 years old in 1970 earned $489 in 1970, their wages increasing sharply to $743 in 1980, then to $849 in 1990. Similarly, the median earnings of the same cohort of immigrants who were born in Japan, Korea, or China increased rapidly from $406 to $821 to $962.

Table 4.1

Median Weekly Earnings of Immigrants by Arrival Cohort of Men 25–34 Years Old in 1970 (in California and the United States, 1970–1990)

Country, Year: Age in Year	Dollars							
	Year of Arrival							
	Before 1950	1950– 1959	1960– 1964	1965– 1969	1970– 1974	1975– 1979	1980– 1984	1985– 1989
In California								
Mexico								
1970: 25–34	470	424	405	320				
1980: 35–44	497	493	453	405	342	263		
1990: 45–54	558	519	423	391	325	288	250	208
Europe								
1970: 25–34	718	640	650	489				
1980: 35–44	854	772	788	743	631	602		
1990: 45–54	923	900	808	849	633	654	738	600
Japan, Korea, China								
1970: 25–34	653	529	513	406				
1980: 35–44	821	748	821	821	598	493		
1990: 45–54	755	923	962	962	673	585	463	382
In the United States								
Mexico								
1970: 25–34	450	405	392	326				
1980: 35–44	492	488	449	400	342	263		
1990: 45–54	519	481	423	385	320	283	250	210
Europe								
1970: 25–34	620	587	587	491				
1980: 35–44	794	711	723	666	586	531		
1990: 45–54	923	769	750	708	596	642	625	600
Japan, Korea, China								
1970: 25–34	587	596	525	385				
1980: 35–44	820	741	847	788	565	493		
1990: 45–54	779	923	962	952	673	577	462	370

NOTE: Earnings are expressed in 1990 dollars.

Although immigrants' real earnings have increased over time, so have the real earnings of native-born workers. As workers increase their labor market experience, it is expected that, in turn, their wages will rise. But most of the concern over the labor market performance of immigrants is whether the differences in earnings between immigrant and native-born workers that exist when immigrants enter the

Table 4.2

Median Weekly Earnings of Immigrant Workers Relative to Those of Native-Born Workers, by Arrival Cohort and Origin for Men 25–34 Years Old in 1970 (in California and the United States, 1970–1990)

	Percentage							
	Year of Arrival							
Country, Year: Age in Year	Before 1950	1950–1959	1960–1964	1965–1969	1970–1974	1975–1979	1980–1984	1985–1989
In California								
Mexico								
1970: 25–34	80	72	68	54				
1980: 35–44	68	68	62	56	47	36		
1990: 45–54	70	65	53	49	41	36	31	26
Europe								
1970: 25–34	122	108	110	83				
1980: 35–44	118	106	109	102	87	83		
1990: 45–54	117	114	102	107	80	82	93	76
Japan, Korea, China								
1970: 25–34	111	90	87	69				
1980: 35–44	113	103	113	113	82	68		
1990: 45–54	95	117	122	121	85	74	58	48
In the United States								
Mexico								
1970: 25–34	86	77	75	62				
1980: 35–44	74	74	68	60	52	40		
1990: 45–54	77	71	62	57	47	42	37	31
Europe								
1970: 25–34	118	112	112	94				
1980: 35–44	120	108	110	101	89	80		
1990: 45–54	137	114	111	105	88	95	92	89
Japan, Korea, China								
1970: 25–34	112	114	100	73				
1980: 35–44	124	112	128	120	85	75		
1990: 45–54	115	137	142	141	100	85	68	54

United States diminish over time. To examine this question, in Table 4.2 we report the median earnings of immigrants *relative* to the median earnings of natives. (The conclusions are unchanged if relative mean earnings are examined.)

Consider the same immigrant cohort of Mexicans in California. In 1970, Mexicans who were 25–34 years old and who entered the United States between 1965 and 1969 earned 54 percent of the earnings of 25–34-year-old native men. By 1980, these men were 35–44 years old, and their earnings relative to 35–44-year-old native men were 56 percent. By 1990, the relative earnings of this group were 49 percent, representing a *decline* in relative earnings of 5 percentage points over the 20-year period. Immigrants of each arrival cohort can be traced in a similar manner.

The relative earnings of the 1950–1959 Mexican immigrant group (72 percent in 1970) are higher than the relative earnings for immigrants arriving between 1965 and 1969 (54 percent in 1970) because, at least in part, the age at which they immigrated was lower. As a result, a greater share of the earlier immigrants attended U.S. schools and reaped the labor market benefits from doing so. However, even among this group of younger-arriving immigrants, the relative earnings decreased from 72 percent in 1970 to 65 percent in 1990.

In sum, the earnings of Mexicans in California and the United States, relative to those of natives of the same age, decreased as the two groups became older; Mexicans did not improve their economic position relative to native workers of the same age.

Immigrants from different countries of origin had fundamentally different patterns of labor market earnings, and the comparison among Mexicans, Europeans, and Japanese, Koreans, and Chinese highlights these disparities. In California, Europeans 25–34 years old in 1970 who arrived between 1965 and 1969 earned 83 percent of what natives earned—higher than the 54 percent for Mexicans and the 69 percent for Japanese, Koreans, and Chinese. Between 1970 and 1980, the relative earnings of these Europeans increased to 102 percent, leaving European immigrants and natives at the same level of earnings. The earnings of this group of European immigrants continued to grow faster than the earnings of natives over the 1980s; by 1990, they were earning 7 percent *more* than native workers who were the same age (i.e., 45–54-year-olds).

The growth in relative earnings among Japanese, Koreans, and Chinese was even greater than that of Europeans. After experiencing relative wages of 69 percent in 1970, the cohort of Japanese, Korean, and Chinese men 25–34 years old in 1970 who entered between 1965 and 1969 had their relative earnings increase to 113 percent in 1980 and continued to experience gains in the 1980s. By 1990 their relative earnings were 121 percent. The patterns for California and the nation were similar.

Multivariate Analyses

The analyses for Mexicans, Europeans, and Japanese, Koreans, and Chinese in Tables 4.1 and 4.2 illustrate the differences in wage growth among immigrants from different countries.[3] To extend these results, we next examine the wage growth for each of the eight country groups in a multivariate context, which enables us to determine whether the disparities in earnings are due to differences in, for example, education. The multivariate methods also allow us to distinguish between the advantages that immigrants gain from general labor market experience—what we call the "experience effect"—and the advantages they gain from experience that is specific to the U.S. labor market, such as learning English and becoming familiar with the process of locating and keeping a job in the United States—what we and previous researchers call "assimilation," because it is associated with the amount of time spent in the United States.

The sum of these two effects equals the change in immigrants' wages as they age, and it is our measure of *economic progress.* To determine the extent to which the gap in wages diminishes over time, we then compare these changes in wages of immigrants with changes in wages of native-born workers as they age.

To disentangle these various effects, we estimate earnings equations for each origin group for both California and the nation as a whole. From these analyses, we present the earnings profiles of each immigrant group in California (Figures 4.1a–h) and the nation (Figures A.1a–h). These profiles represent the path of earnings of an immigrant who entered the United States at age 25, demonstrating the change in wages for immigrants and natives as they age: the sum of the experience effect and the assimilation effect. To demonstrate the

---

[3]The ninth group, Indochina and Vietnam, was not included, because the majority of this group only began emigrating after 1970.

magnitude of the assimilation effect, we also report the earnings profiles of immigrants as if they had received no gains from U.S.–specific experience (i.e., as if the assimilation effect were zero). (The Appendix details the multivariate analyses that were conducted and the calculations that were the basis of the earnings profiles displayed in the figures.)

Immigrants from Mexico and Central America have similar, low earnings profiles (Figures 4.1a and b). They receive substantially lower wages at the time of entry than natives. Moreover, the rate of wage growth is very low, although it is higher for Central Americans than it is for Mexicans. As a result, the earnings difference persists over the workers' working lives. In fact, the absolute wage gap between Mexican immigrants and natives actually increases somewhat as the workers get older. Moreover, the assimilation effect is quite small for Mexicans, causing only a modest increase in their earnings.

Filipino immigrants are much more educated than Mexican or Central American immigrants; therefore, their earnings are also much higher. However, their earnings do not grow as fast as those of natives (over most of the age range). As a result, the earnings gap between them and natives increases at older ages.

Immigrants from the UK, Canada, and Europe start out with earnings that are only slightly lower than the earnings of natives of the same age, and within 5 to 10 years they earn just as much or more than natives, on average (Figures 4.1d and e). Somewhat surprisingly, immigrants from the UK and Canada have very high rates of assimilation. We hypothesized that these immigrants would not have high rates of assimilation because they already speak English. This evidence suggests that assimilation consists of more than just learning English.

Immigrants from Japan, Korea, and China experience a pattern of earnings growth that is distinct from that of both Europeans and Mexicans. Upon arrival, they have wages that are substantially lower than natives of the same age. However, these immigrants have extraordinarily high rates of wage growth following their arrival in the United States. Within 7 to 12 years they have the same wages as natives. Moreover, most of the wage growth is due to the assimilation effect; without assimilation, these immigrants would achieve modest increases in earnings.

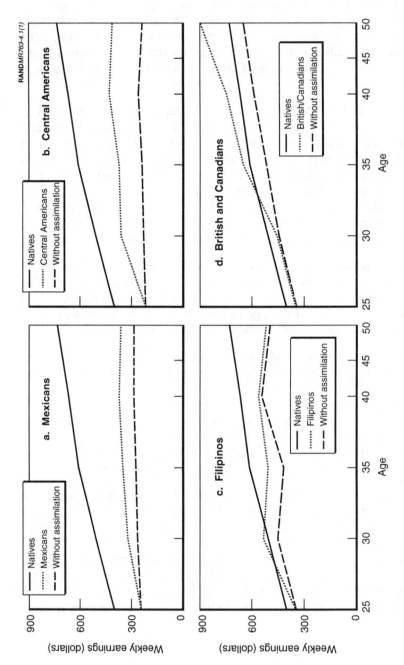

Figure 4.1—Earnings Profiles of Immigrants in California (With and Without Assimilation Effects)

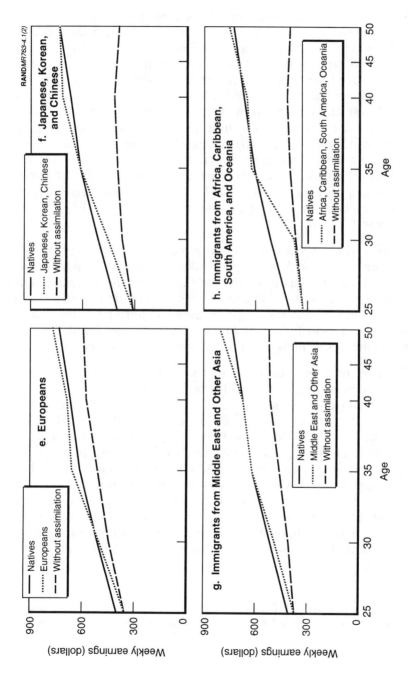

Figure 4.1—continued

In sum, when immigrants from Europe enter the U.S. labor market, they begin earning wages that are only slightly lower than those of natives of the same age. In general, their earnings relative to those of natives improve somewhat over time, so they quickly reach parity with native-born workers. At the time they enter the U.S. labor market, immigrants from Japan, Korea, and China earn wages that are lower than those of newly arrived European immigrants. However, the earnings of Japanese, Korean, and Chinese immigrants increase rapidly; within approximately 10 years they are earning wages that are at least as great as natives' wages. The experience of Mexicans, whose relative wages are low at entry and do not increase the longer they stay in the United States, contrasts starkly with the experience of the Europeans and of the Japanese, Koreans, and Chinese.

Finally, whereas some immigrant groups experience high levels of assimilation, some do not. Specifically, immigrants from the UK and Canada, Europe, Japan, Korea, and China, and the Middle East and other Asian countries have high rates of assimilation while immigrants from Mexico and the Philippines do not. To further explore factors that contribute to assimilation, we analyze next the role that attending U.S. schools has in increasing labor market earnings.

The Role of Attending U.S. Schools. The immigrants examined in the analyses arrived in the United States at a variety of ages. Kossoudji (1988), Friedberg (1991), and Borjas (1995) documented that earnings are higher among those who enter the United States at younger ages.[4] In addition, Friedberg (1991) demonstrates that among labor force participants, the distribution of age at arrival is related to the length of time spent in the United States: Those labor force participants who have not been in the United States many years are more likely to have immigrated as adults because child immigrants are not yet in the labor force; similarly, among those who have been in the United States several years, the immigrants who arrived as adults are more likely to have already retired and not be in the labor force.

---

[4]Baker and Benjamin (1994) also examined the sensitivity of their estimates of assimilation to age at migration in Canada by excluding those who arrived before age 16.

The primary behavioral explanation for the negative relationship be-tween age at migration and earnings is that immigrants who arrive at young ages are more likely to be educated in U.S. schools, and the skills they learn in U.S. schools are valued in the U.S. labor market. In fact, among the entire sample of immigrant men considered in California (not just the sample of 25–34-year-old men reported in Table 4.3), 26 percent attended a U.S. school.[5] The same rate in the nation is 27 percent. Therefore, over one-quarter of all adult im-migrants are influenced by American schools.

To investigate the importance of immigrants' being educated in the United States, in Table 4.3 for each origin group, we report the aver-age weekly wages, years of education, and age for those immigrants who attended U.S. schools and those who did not. Although immi-grants who attended U.S. schools are younger, on average, they have substantially higher earnings, partly because they are more highly educated. For example, Mexican immigrants who were educated in

---

[5]We assume that an immigrant attended a U.S. school if the age at which he stopped schooling (for the last time) was greater than the age at which he migrated. Because the exact date of migration is not ascertained in the censuses, we estimate it as current age (A) minus the midpoint of the range of years since migration (YSM). For example, for someone who migrated 0–5 years prior to the census, YSM equals 2.5. For the open-ended range of 30 or more years since arrival, YSM is assumed to equal 35. Because just 11.5 percent of immigrants nationally falls into this open-ended range, the measurement error induced by the necessary approximation is not likely to be substantial. Age at school leaving is calculated as the years of schooling plus seven, which implicitly assumes that immigrants begin schooling at age seven. Assuming age seven instead of age six, which has been done in many previous studies of the effects of labor market experience, also reflects the fact that a nontrivial share of immigrants repeats at least one grade. This assumption is likely to categorize some workers who did not attend U.S. schools as having done so, thereby leading to an underestimate of the difference in earnings between those educated and not educated in the United States. Although single years of schooling are reported in the 1970 and 1980 Censuses, they were not in 1990. In calculating the age at which the immigrant left school using the 1990 Census, we assumed the following years of schooling for each reported schooling group: none equals zero, kindergarten or nursery school equals 0.5, 0–4 equals 2.5, 5–8 equals 6.5, high school degree or GED equals 12, some college equals 13, associate's degree equals 14, bachelor's degree equals 16, and advanced degree equals 17. Park (1994) uses a comparable procedure, but he considers those who ob-tained no more than six years of schooling abroad as being educated in the United States, which implicitly defines all other immigrants, including those who came to the United States for undergraduate and graduate school, as not having been educated in the United States. He estimates that 24.4 percent (Table 5) of male immigrants 25–34 years old in 1980 had been educated in the United States, which, as expected, is lower than our estimate (using all immigrants 25 to 60 years old in the merged 1970, 1980, and 1990 Census) of the number who ever attended U.S. schools.

Table 4.3

Weekly Earnings, Education, and Age Differences Between Those Immigrants Who Were Educated in the United States and Those Who Were Not (National Estimates)

Country of Origin	Average Weekly Earnings ($)		Average Years of Education		Average Age (years)		Number of Observations	
	Educated in U.S.	Not Educated in U.S.	Educated in U.S.	Not Educated in U.S.	Educated in U.S.	Not Educated in U.S.	Educated in U.S.	Not Educated in U.S.
Mexico	497	382	11.7	6.4	32.5	37.7	12,148	47,879
Japan, Korea, China	788	698	15.3	13.4	35.0	40.8	4686	12,983
Central America	580	394	13.3	9.0	32.8	36.4	1992	8106
Philippines	666	618	14.1	13.5	34.6	41.5	2904	8587
Europe	807	715	13.7	10.6	38.5	46.0	11,546	21,995
Middle East, Other Asia	868	770	15.5	14.0	34.3	40.1	4741	10,470
Africa, Caribbean, South Africa, Oceania	706	587	14.2	11.8	33.9	41.6	6495	17,194
UK, Canada	787	838	13.7	12.5	38.8	45.4	5853	9457
Natives	673		12.5		40.1		1,628,190	

NOTE: Includes all men in the sample for the multivariate analyses using the 1970, 1980, and 1990 Census data.

the United States have almost double the number of years of schooling (11.7) of those who did not (6.4). An exception is the group of immigrants from the UK and Canada. Those educated abroad have higher wages; however, this group of immigrants is also almost seven years older, on average, than those who were educated in the United States.

The share of workers in our sample who did not attend U.S. schools varies also across origin groups. The highest share is for Mexicans (79 percent) and Central Americans (80 percent), and the lowest share is for British and Canadians (62 percent) and Europeans (66 percent).[6] This difference, combined with the fact that immigrants educated in the United States earn substantially higher wages, may explain the disparities in earnings across groups; we address these disparities below.

Even though the earnings of immigrants not educated in the United States are generally lower than the earnings of those who were, perhaps this gap in earnings diminishes the longer that immigrants stay in the United States. We examine this issue first by replicating the analyses displayed in Table 4.2. But instead of reporting the weekly wages of immigrants relative to those of natives, we report the weekly wages of immigrants not schooled in the United States relative to the weekly wages of immigrants who *did* attend U.S. schools. Because of the small sample sizes, especially for California, Table 4.4 reports results for all immigrants combined. We find that the size of the difference in earnings between these two immigrant groups increases substantially the longer the immigrants remain in the United States. The 91-percent earnings ratio among immigrants 25–34 years old in 1970 who arrived in the United States between 1950 and 1959 decreased to 72 percent by 1980 and to 56 percent in 1990. The patterns for California and the nation are similar, and they underscore the importance of distinguishing between those who did and did not attend U.S. schools.

To compare the earnings profiles of these two groups more directly with the profiles for all immigrants, we reestimated the national re-

---

[6]Among immigrants, the percentage not attending U.S. schools is 73 from Japan, Korea, and China; 74 from Philippines; 69 from Middle East and other Asian countries; and 72 from Africa, Caribbean, South America, and Oceania.

Table 4.4

Median Weekly Earnings of Immigrants Who Were Educated in the United States Relative to Those of Immigrants Who Were Not, by Arrival Cohort (Men 25–34 Years Old in 1970, California and the Nation)

Year: Age in Year (Number of Observations)[a]	Percentage			
	Year of Arrival			
	Before 1950	1950– 1959	1960– 1964	1965– 1969
In California				
1970: 25–34 (1540, 844)	—[b]	91	93	81
1980: 35–44 (9243, 2820)	—[b]	72	75	61
1990: 45–54 (12,489, 2485)	53	56	62	55
In the Nation				
1970: 25–34 (2138, 3959)	—[b]	90	92	106
1980: 35–44 (14,026, 4660)	—[b]	72	77	65
1990: 45–54 (17,891, 3981)	50	58	60	56

[a]In parentheses is the number of observations used to calculate the median earnings for immigrants who did not attend U.S. schools and for those who did, respectively.

[b]There were fewer than 50 observations in the given category for either the numerator or denominator.

gressions reported in Table A.7 separately for those immigrants who did and did not attend U.S. schools. From these regressions, we depict the earnings profiles in the same way that we did to generate Figures 4.1a–h, for those who were and were not educated in the United States (Figures 4.2a–h).[7]

Mexicans and Central Americans who attended U.S. schools had substantially higher earnings profiles than those who did not, and the gap between these immigrants and natives decreased substantially as the workers aged. In fact, Central Americans educated in the United States have earnings profiles similar to natives—not surpris-

---

[7]Comparing those who did and did not attend a U.S. school is somewhat similar empirically to comparing those who arrived before, say, their 18th birthday with those who arrived after it. (Borjas, 1995, uses age 18 as the cutoff for immigration as an adult.) Nationally, only 6.1 percent of the sample who were not schooled in the United States arrived in the United States before age 18, and 16 percent of those who arrived before age 18 were not schooled in the United States. As a result, the problem of differences in age at migration across arrival cohorts observed among adults in the labor force, as pointed out by Friedberg (1991), is substantially mitigated in these analyses.

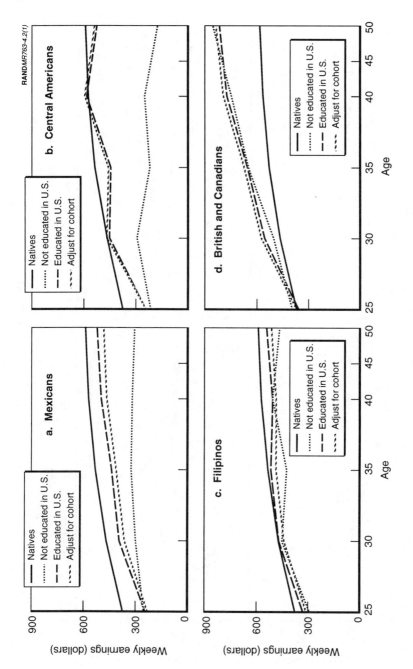

Figure 4.2—Earnings Profiles by Whether Educated in the United States (for United States as a Whole)

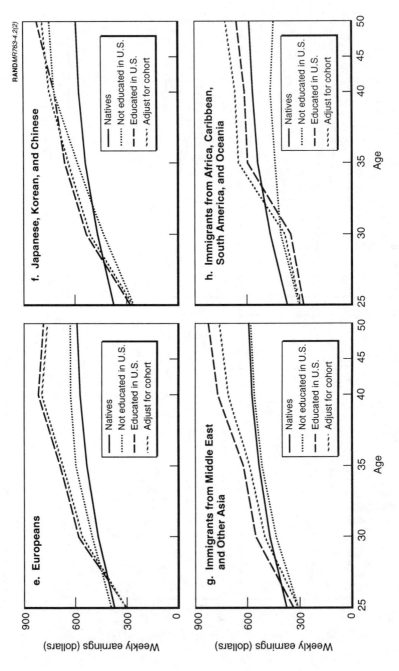

Figure 4.2—continued

ing, given their almost one full year more of education than natives, on average (Table 4.3). This pattern is not true for immigrants from the United Kingdom and Canada, the Philippines, or Japan, Korea, and China, because the largest differences in completed education between those who did and did not attend U.S. schools were for Mexicans and Central Americans, perhaps because the quality of schooling in Mexico and Central America is lower than it is in the United States.

One explanation for the differences in profiles is that those immigrants who arrived as children were more likely to immigrate in earlier rather than more-recent periods (not shown here), and at least for some immigrant groups, more-recent arrivals have fared worse (i.e., the cohort effects have become negative and larger more recently). We investigate this issue by displaying the earnings profiles for immigrants who attended U.S. schools but assuming that they arrived during the same period as immigrants (of that same origin group) who did not attend U.S. schools (Figures 4.2a–h). In general, adjusting for cohort of arrival lowers the earnings profiles of these workers. However, the primary patterns are not affected by the cohort patterns of arrival.

Changes in the "Quality" of Immigrants. Partly in response to the change in immigration policy in 1965, which placed more emphasis on family reunification and less on immigrant skills, several studies have tried to examine whether the labor market skills and abilities—i.e., "quality"—of immigrants have diminished since 1965. Examining the changes in educational attainment of immigrants (relative to those of natives) for more- versus less-recently arrived immigrants, such studies have found a substantial decline in relative attainment (Borjas, 1995; Funkhauser and Trejo, 1995). In addition, several studies have examined the change in "quality" as defined by labor market earnings adjusted for differences in, for example, education, age, or country of origin (Borjas, 1985; LaLonde and Topel, 1992; Funkhauser and Trejo, 1995). Our analyses provide additional evidence on this latter measure of "quality," and it is represented by the effects of the year-of-arrival indicators in the multivariate analyses (Tables A.7 and A.8).

The changes in "quality" vary substantially across immigrants; patterns are similar in California and the nation. More-recent

Mexican immigrants are of substantially lower "quality" than earlier Mexican arrivals. After controlling for age and education, we found that those arriving from 1985 to 1990 earned 41 percent lower wages than those immigrants who arrived between 1960 and 1965.[8] Filipino immigrants experienced a similar pattern of decreasing "quality," both in California and in the nation. At the same time, the "quality" of immigrants from Japan, Korea, and China has increased substantially in California,[9] and earnings of those arriving in the late 1980s are 25 percent higher than the earnings of those arriving in the early 1960s.[10]

Whereas previous studies (e.g., Borjas, 1995) have combined all Asian immigrants, finding that the "quality" of these immigrants has decreased over time, our results indicate that Asians are a heterogeneous group, the "quality" increasing among some groups and decreasing among others. The coefficient estimates for Central American immigrants suggest decreasing "quality"; however, the differences are much smaller than those for Mexicans or Filipinos, and the estimates are imprecise. Immigrants from Europe and from the Middle East and other Asian countries have not experienced substantial changes in "quality. "

---

[8]Forty-one percent is the exponentiated coefficient in Table A.7, i.e., $e^{0.341}$.

[9]The "quality" of the immigrants from Japan, Korea, and China has not increased nationally, however.

[10]Except for immigrants from Central America, the substantive results are the same when immigrants schooled in the United States are excluded. Using more-aggregated country groupings, Friedberg (1991) found that the decline in immigrant "quality" over time is mitigated once age at arrival is controlled for. However, our finding that the estimated "quality" does not change substantially when examining just those educated abroad is consistent with Borjas' (1995) result that estimated "quality" does not change when he controls for age at migration. But Borjas did not examine Central Americans per se, so he did not find our result for this immigrant group. For the nation, the number of Central Americans in the regressions dropped from 10,098 to 8106 when immigrants schooled in the United States were excluded. The coefficients estimates (standard error) on the year of entry indicators for 1985–1990, 1980–1984, 1975–1979, 1970–1974, 1960–1964, 1950–1959, and before 1950 are, respectively, –.80 (.35), –.89 (.36), –.40 (.18), –.47 (.19), –.01 (.08), .38 (.18), and .72 (.34). These estimates imply a much greater decrease in "quality" than those in Table A.7, which includes those schooled in the United States, suggesting that more-recent immigrants are more likely to have been schooled in the United States than were earlier Central American immigrants.

EDUCATION AND LIFETIME ECONOMIC PROGRESS

Educational attainment is an important determinant of labor market earnings, and it differs markedly among immigrant groups and natives. In this section, we determine the extent to which the earnings disparities are explained by differences in years of schooling—the second question of interest.

While 57 percent of natives have more than a high school degree, only 26 percent of Central Americans and 12 percent of Mexicans have this level of schooling (Table 4.5). Immigrants from these two groups are concentrated in the lowest education categories. Thirty-five percent of Central Americans and 59 percent of Mexicans have less than nine years of schooling.

At the same time, immigrants from Europe, the UK and Canada, and the combined group of Africa, Caribbean, South America, and Oceania have education levels that are very similar to those of native-born workers. And immigrants from Japan, Korea, and China, the

Table 4.5

Distribution of Completed Years of Schooling for Each Origin Group, 25–60-Year-Old Men in California, Combined 1970, 1980, and 1990

Country of Origin	Percentage Years of Schooling								
	0–4	5–8	9	10	11	12	13–15	16	17+
Mexico	26.2	32.5	6.1	3.4	3.3	16.3	8.9	1.7	1.6
Japan, Korea, China	3.6	5.1	2.4	1.1	1.2	17.9	20.5	25.4	22.7
Central America	13.2	21.4	7.8	3.2	3.6	24.5	18.5	4.5	3.2
Philippines	1.7	3.4	1.0	2.5	1.3	18.3	32.5	28.7	10.5
Europe	4.0	11.2	2.4	3.3	2.3	23.7	22.9	13.1	17.1
Middle East, Other Asia	2.0	3.3	1.1	1.8	1.4	16.0	21.2	23.4	29.9
Africa, Caribbean, South America, Oceania	2.3	6.7	2.1	2.1	2.4	23.6	29.5	14.9	16.4
UK, Canada	0.5	4.1	2.4	4.4	3.9	26.6	27.3	14.7	16.1
Natives	0.9	4.1	2.3	3.5	3.9	28.2	29.2	15.0	13.0

Philippines, and the Middle East and other Asian countries have educational levels that exceed those of native-born workers; for each of these immigrant groups, approximately 70 percent of the male workers have more than a high school diploma. And among the Japanese, Koreans, and Chinese, nearly one out of every four workers has more than a bachelor's degree; for immigrants from the Middle East and other Asian countries, approximately 30 percent has this high level of schooling.

Do Disparities in Completed Education Explain Differences in Earnings Profiles?

Given the large differences in completed education, we next examine the extent to which disparities in years of schooling explain the differences in earnings profiles. We have estimated the earnings profiles of each immigrant group, assuming that they had the same education distribution as natives. The results of these analyses are similar for California (Figures 4.3a–h and 4.4) and the nation (Figures A.2 and A.3); therefore, we discuss only the results for California.

A significant share of the difference in the earnings profile between Mexicans and natives—approximately one-third—is explained by the substantial difference in educational attainment. However, even if immigrants had completed the same number of years of school as natives, a significant earnings gap would remain between Mexicans and natives. To assess whether that gap exists at high levels of education, we examined the difference for Mexicans with 16 years of schooling and found that even the highly educated Mexicans have substantially lower earnings than the *average* native (Figure 4.4).

Disparities in years of schooling also explain some of the gap between natives and Central Americans. However, adjusting for differences in educational attainment among immigrants from the United Kingdom and Canada, Africa, the Caribbean, South America, and Oceania, Europe, Japan, Korea, and China, and the Philippines changes the earnings profiles very little, because these groups have relatively similar years of completed schooling to those of native-born workers.

If differences in completed education do not explain all the wage gap, then what does? There are several potential explanations. As

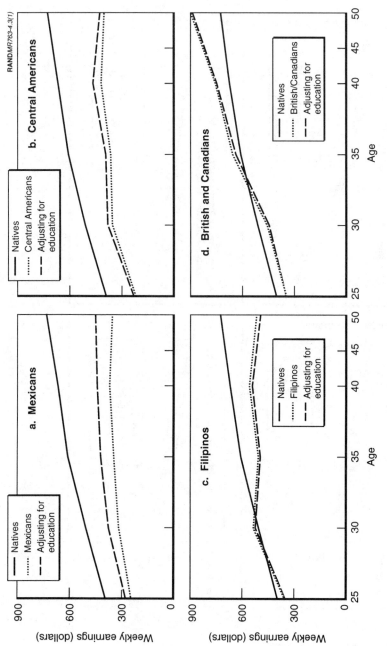

Figure 4.3—Earnings Profiles With and Without Adjusting for Differences in Education, California

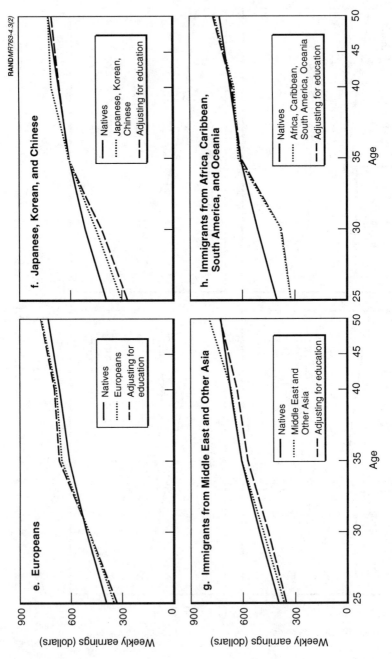

RAND*MR763-4.3(2)*

e. Europeans

f. Japanese, Korean, and Chinese

g. Immigrants from Middle East and Other Asia

h. Immigrants from Africa, Caribbean, South America, and Oceania

Figure 4.3—continued

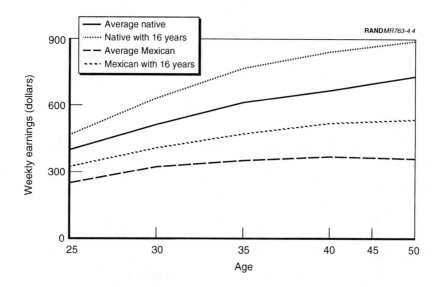

**Figure 4.4—Earnings Profiles for Mexicans and Natives with
Various Levels of Education (With and Without
Adjusting for Differences), California**

emphasized by LaLonde and Topel (1991), the decreasing returns to
education in the United States have negatively influenced the labor
market progress of immigrants. Table 4.6 reports the returns to education for natives and for each immigrant group separately by
whether they were educated in the United States.[11] The returns to
education among natives increased from .079 to .103 between 1970
and 1990. At the same time, returns to education among Mexican
immigrants educated in Mexico declined from .038 to just .022.
Combined with the decline in education of Mexicans relative to that
of natives (Smith, unpublished), these trends have contributed to the
low growth rate in earnings of Mexicans. Borjas (1995) estimated
that these changes in the wage structure explain 17 percent of the de-

---

[11]Park (1994), who examined 25–34-year-old men, obtained similar results for
Mexicans, except that his estimate for returns to schooling among U.S.–educated
Mexicans in 1990 is somewhat higher (.081). Similarly, his estimate for all immigrants
combined is similar to ours, except that his 1990 estimate for immigrants schooled in
the United States (.091) is larger.

Table 4.6

Returns to Schooling by Whether Educated in the United States, 1970, 1980, and 1990, for the Nation

Country of Origin	Returns (percentage)					
	1970		1980		1990	
	U.S. Schooling	No U.S. Schooling	U.S. Schooling	No U.S. Schooling	U.S. Schooling	No U.S. Schooling
All	6.0	4.5	5.6	5.1	5.7	5.3
Mexico	6.4	3.8	4.0	2.9	5.3	2.2
Japan, Korea, China	10.7	4.7	8.6	5.7	13.1	6.6
Central America	4.8	3.1	5.5	3.7	8.1	2.8
Philippines	6.6	5.4	7.5	5.1	7.9	6.5
Europe	6.2	3.7	6.6	4.1	8.2	4.6
Middle East, Other Asia	4.0	4.7	7.1	5.1	12.5	6.3
Africa, Caribbean, South America, Oceania	4.7	3.6	6.4	5.1	10.0	5.9
UK, Canada	5.6	4.1	4.8	5.2	8.3	6.5
Natives	7.9		7.1		10.3	

NOTE: Estimates are based on models identical to those in Table A.7, except that education is specified as linear (in logs) and it is not interacted with age. The returns to schooling are allowed to vary among 1970, 1980, and 1990, both for immigrants and for natives separately.

cline in immigrant relative wages (among all origin groups as a whole) between 1970 and 1990.

The increase in labor market earnings that results from attending U.S. schools, as depicted in Figures 4.2a–h, occurs, in part, because of the increase in labor market earnings associated with an additional year of schooling—i.e., the returns to schooling are higher for immigrants educated in the United States. In fact, we find that this is true for immigrants from all countries in all years (Table 4.6),[12] which is consistent with Smith's (unpublished) findings for Hispanics and Park's (1994) findings for more broadly defined immigrant groups.

---

[12]The only exception is in 1980 for immigrants from the United Kingdom and Canada.

Moreover, even among immigrants attending U.S. schools, the returns to schooling (i.e., the percentage change in earnings associated with increase in schooling by 1 year) vary substantially across immigrant groups. In 1990, Mexicans had the lowest returns, 5.3 percent; most other groups had returns of about 8.0 percent or more; and immigrants from Japan, Korea, and China experienced returns of 13.1 percent. These disparities are likely due to differences in the quality of education among these groups.

A second reason for differences in earnings profiles among immigrant groups is that they have arrived at times of greater or lesser economic growth. Those who arrive in prosperous times experience greater labor market success, perhaps. However, the two groups with the most distinct patterns of economic progress, i.e., Mexicans and Japanese, Koreans, and Chinese, arrived in the United States at similar times. In fact, a slightly greater share of Japanese, Koreans, and Chinese arrived more recently than Mexicans, and Mexicans arriving more recently have done substantially worse than Mexicans who came to the United States during earlier periods.[13] Therefore, adjusting for cohort of arrival between Mexicans and Japanese, Koreans, and Chinese would make the differences in earnings appear even larger.

Although the analyses adjust for education, they do not adjust for English-language ability. Smith (unpublished), McManus, Gould, and Welch (1983), Grenier (1984), Kossoudji (1988), and Funkhauser (1995a,b), found that there are significant returns to English skills, which suggests that these skills are a third reason for the remaining disparity in wages.

A fourth reason for the remaining differences in earnings profiles is that immigrants receive different returns to experience.

Fifth, illegal immigrants may receive lower wages because of the risk to employers of hiring them. That is, to make it profitable to take the chance of being punished for hiring illegal immigrants, the cost of hiring illegal workers must be lower than the cost of hiring similarly

---

[13]The percentage of Mexicans versus Japanese, Koreans, and Chinese arriving in the 1960s, 1970s, and 1990s was 24.2 versus 32.1, 37.4 versus 35.3, and 20.9 versus 20.6, respectively.

qualified legal immigrants or native workers. That cost translates into lower wages for illegal immigrants. Using estimates by Borjas and Tienda (1989), we can see that the wage penalty for being undocumented may be as high as 7–10 percent.[14] Moreover, the number of undocumented immigrants—an estimated 1,552,000 in California alone in 1994 (Fernandez and Robinson, 1994)—is substantial. A disproportionate number are from Mexico.[15]

Sixth, immigrant workers may suffer from "enclave effects," whereby a high geographic concentration of similarly skilled immigrant workers suppresses the wages of immigrants in the enclave.

Seventh, unexplored cultural differences in attitudes toward work may explain some of the differences.

Eighth, discrimination of selected immigrant groups may drive a wedge between their wages and the wages of equally skilled native workers.

In sum, there are a variety of reasons that wage differences may persist even after differences in completed education are adjusted for. Future research will undoubtedly address this issue.

Does Assimilation Vary by Education Level?

Education may not only have a direct effect on earnings, as examined above; it may also have an effect on the ability of immigrants to assimilate. The process of assimilation includes learning a new language and learning how the U.S. labor market functions. We hypothesize that assimilation may be more rapid for those with more education because they have the ability to learn these skills more quickly. For example, Mexicans may have a relatively low rate of assimilation because, as a group, they have lower educational attainment. However it may be that well-educated Mexicans experience high rates of assimilation. On the other hand, highly

---

[14]This estimate is based on Borjas and Tienda's (1989, p. 735) estimate that at least three-quarters of the 30-percent wage penalty may be accounted for by differences in country of origin and age between legal and undocumented immigrants.

[15]This estimate is the average of Fernandez and Robinson's (1994) high and low estimates.

educated immigrants are more likely than less-educated immigrants to enter the country with some knowledge of English; therefore, those who are less educated have the opportunity to reap the largest benefits from learning the language. In addition, this hypothesis would suggest that we would be less likely to find differential rates of assimilation across education groups among those immigrants arriving from countries such as Canada and the United Kingdom, whose language is English.

We tested this hypothesis in the multivariate analyses. The assimilation rates for those with less than 12 years of schooling, those with exactly 12 years of schooling, and those with more than 12 years of schooling are reported in Table 4.7 for the nation. Because selective cross-state migration may bias the estimates for California, and because the results are somewhat different between the United States and California, we discuss the results for the nation. The results for California are in Table A.4. Also note that a series of statistical tests were conducted to determine whether there were statistically significant differences in the rates of assimilation across education groups. We discuss only the instances for which the differences were statistically significant. A discussion of the tests that were made is contained in the Appendix, and the results of the tests are reported in Tables A.5 and A.6.

Statistically significant and substantively important differences were found among education groups for some country groups. For Mexicans, the evidence suggests that the more-educated workers assimilate more quickly: After 15 to 20 years, Mexicans with less than 12 years of schooling experienced a 14-percent earnings growth from assimilation; those with more than 12 years of schooling experienced a 22-percent earnings growth—more than a 50-percent higher rate of assimilation. After 30 or more years of assimilation, the difference is 75 percent (i.e., [26.2 – 15.0]/15.0).

Just the opposite relationship is found for immigrants from the UK, Canada, and Europe: Those who have completed fewer years of schooling assimilate more rapidly. For the UK and Canada, after 10 to 15 years the wages of those with less than 12 years of schooling have increased by 26 percent; the change in wages of those with

Table 4.7

Percentage[a] Gain in Weekly Earnings Relative to Being in the United States Less Than Five Years, for Each Origin and Schooling Group, for the Nation

Percentage

Number of Years in United States	Mexico (20.4%)[b] Years of Education			Japan/Korea/China (7.9%)[b] Years of Education		
	Less than 12	12 Years	More than 12	Less than 12	12 Years	More than 12
5–10	12.6	14.3	10.8	25.5	19.5	20.9
10–15	14.6	15.7	17.8	36.5	28.5	30.6
15–20	14.4	19.7	21.6	49.2	36.7	43.0
20–30	17.2	16.3	21.7	52.8	43.3	51.9
30 or more	15.0	20.8	26.2	71.6	66.9	70.7

Number of Years in United States	Central America (4.0%)[b] Years of Education			Philippines (4.3%)[b] Years of Education		
	Less than 12	12 Years	More than 12	Less than 12	12 Years	More than 12
5–10	29.3	24.3	31.5	27.0	18.0	24.1
10–15	18.8	12.9	15.7	7.8	8.8	16.5
15–20	32.8	29.5	35.1	20.1	5.3	22.1
20–30	33.4	23.5	23.1	15.3	6.7	13.6
30 or more	28.4	24.2	27.2	2.7	-4.3	-5.4

Table 4.7—continued

Percentage

Number of Years in United States	Europe (24.5%)[b]			Middle East, Other Asia (8.3%)[b]		
	Years of Education			Years of Education		
	Less than 12	12 Years	More than 12	Less than 12	12 Years	More than 12
5–10	14.7	16.7	8.5	23.2	14.7	16.6
10–15	22.4	17.6	16.4	40.6	15.3	29.2
15–20	24.4	18.9	18.1	30.1	15.7	32.4
20–30	29.8	18.7	19.9	50.6	39.2	42.0
30 or more	23.5	17.2	18.6	51.8	43.4	48.6

Number of Years in United States	Africa, Caribbean, South America, Oceania (18.6%)[b]			UK/Canada (9.6%)[b]		
	Years of Education			Years of Education		
	Less than 12	12 Years	More than 12	Less than 12	12 Years	More than 12
5–10	9.8	7.8	7.5	10.7	0.5	4.2
10–15	23.5	22.1	27.0	25.7	10.4	11.0
15–20	22.1	23.1	25.1	29.4	13.6	16.3
20–30	38.6	30.4	37.1	37.2	23.9	22.1
30 or more	44.4	43.7	45.4	34.9	28.8	29.2

[a]Percentage difference is based on the log approximation.

[b]Number in parentheses is the percent of immigrants in the sample who are from the given country of origin. Results for California are reported in Table A.4.

more than 12 years of schooling is only 11 percent. Similarly, the wage growth associated with being in the United States 20–30 years is 37 percent among the least educated and 22 percent among the most educated. Although Europeans have lower rates of assimilation than the British and Canadians, it is also true of Europeans that the least-educated immigrants assimilate more quickly. After 20–30 years, wage growth of those with less than 12 years of schooling is 30 percent, which is 50 percent higher than the growth among European immigrants with more than 12 years of schooling.

The different patterns for immigrants from Mexico and the UK and Canada are consistent with the hypothesis that learning English is an important component of assimilation among immigrants who do not speak the language, and that the most-educated workers are the workers who are able to most quickly learn English. Immigrants from the UK and Canada, all of whom speak English (except possibly some French-speaking Canadians), do not need to learn English; therefore, the least educated are not at a disadvantage and they achieve just as high or, in this case, higher rates of assimilation. However, more highly educated immigrants from countries other than Mexico do not appear to assimilate more quickly than less-educated immigrants from those same countries.[16]

CHANGE IN THE RATE OF ECONOMIC PROGRESS

We now turn to the third question of interest: Has the rate of economic progress changed over the 20-year period from 1970 to 1990? Given the changes in immigrant flows over the past 10 to 15 years, many sectors of the labor market have become dominated by immigrants, which may have created increased competition for jobs. At the same time, returns to education have increased even though immigrants are disproportionately represented in lower-skilled jobs. As a result, immigrants may be finding it more difficult to assimilate into the labor market. This issue may be particularly salient for

---

[16]When we restrict to those immigrants not educated in the United States, we find similar results for immigrants from Mexico, UK and Canada, and Europe. The rates are higher among Filipinos and among Japanese, Koreans, and Chinese; for example, among the latter group, after 30 years the wage difference is 89 percent instead of 67 percent. The rates for immigrants from the Middle East and other Asians countries, and from Africa, Caribbean, South America, and Oceania are substantially lower.

Mexican immigrants, because, as we have shown, they have experienced low rates of wage growth.

The evidence suggests that the rate at which the gap between immigrants and natives has decreased has not improved for Mexicans. We find that the pattern of change in relative wages is quite similar between immigrants of similar ages who arrived in the late 1960s versus the late 1970s (Table 4.8). Consider Mexicans who immigrated between the ages of 25 and 34. Those who immigrated between 1965 and 1969 had relative earnings in 1970 of 54 percent, and those who immigrated between 1975 and 1979 had relative earnings in 1980 of 50 percent. In the subsequent 10 years, those who immigrated dur-

Table 4.8

Relative Median Weekly Earnings of Immigrant and Native-Born Workers for Earlier Versus More-Recent Arrivals (for Immigrants Arriving at Ages 25–34, by Country of Origin, in California, 1970–1990)

Country of Origin, Date of Arrival	Percentage		
	1970	1980	1990
	In California		
Mexico			
Early arrivals: 1965–1969	54	56	50
Late arrivals: 1975–1979	—	50	45
Europe			
Early arrivals: 1965–1969	83	103	108
Late arrivals: 1975–1979	—	87	110
Japan, Korea, China			
Early arrivals: 1965–1969	69	114	122
Late arrivals: 1975–1979	—	75	104
	In the United States		
Mexico			
Early arrivals: 1965–1969	63	61	57
Late arrivals: 1975–1979	—	52	50
Europe			
Early arrivals: 1965–1969	94	101	105
Late arrivals: 1975–1979	—	90	110
Japan, Korea, China			
Early arrivals: 1965–1969	74	120	141
Late arrivals: 1975–1979	—	78	115

ing the late 1960s had relative wages that increased to 56 percent; those who immigrated in the late 1970s had relative wages that *decreased* to 45 percent, suggesting that the rate of assimilation may have declined for more-recent arrivals. However, the relative wages of the earlier arrivals also decreased between 1980 and 1990, from 56 to 50 percent, which suggests that assimilation declined in the 1980s for all Mexican immigrants, not just more-recent arrivals. However, if assimilation declines with age, then one would expect lower rates of assimilation between 1980 and 1990 for the earlier arrivals. Moreover, the results are also consistent with a differential period effect, which was more harmful to Mexicans than to natives, perhaps because of changes in the returns to skills. For whatever reason, however, the rate of economic progress has not improved for more-recent immigrants. This pattern is similar for the nation as well.

The rate of economic progress has not declined for Europeans, either for immigrants in California, or the nation. Moreover, Europeans continue to reach parity with native-born workers within the first 10 years after arriving in the United States. In addition, the patterns suggest that the rate of economic progress may be higher at younger ages, because the rate of progress between 1980 and 1990 is higher for the younger immigrants, especially for the national estimates: The relative wages shortly after arrival were actually lower for the more-recent arrivals than for those who arrived in the late 1960s. Of course, because of confounding age, period, and cohort effects, this relationship cannot be determined definitively.

Economic progress declined somewhat for Japanese, Koreans, and Chinese. In California, the rate of economic progress in the first 10 years after arriving in the United States declined from 45 percentage points (i.e., 114 minus 69) to 29 percentage points (104 minus 75). A decline also occurred for the nation as a whole, although at a smaller scale. However, even with the decline, immigrants from Japan, Korea, and China still reached parity with native-born workers in less than 10 years.

Chapter Five

DISCUSSION

Does the economic well-being of immigrants improve substantially over time, or are most immigrants' wages, which are relatively low when they enter the country, stagnant throughout their working lives?

The earnings of virtually all immigrant groups do, in fact, increase as the workers age; however, the rate at which that growth occurs varies substantially among immigrants arriving from different countries. Europeans have entered with relatively high wages and have earned wages comparable to those of natives over their working lives. Japanese, Koreans, and Chinese have entered with lower wages but have quickly caught up with native-born workers. Mexicans, on the other hand, have entered with low wages, and the wage gap between them and native-born workers has not shrunk. Central Americans have had experience somewhat similar to that of Mexicans. These latter two groups currently constitute 50 percent of immigrants in California.

Education is an important factor in explaining the disparities in earnings profiles among immigrants from different countries, because labor market earnings are closely linked to education and because immigrants arrive with distinct skills and abilities. Higher-educated immigrants have higher wages. And for immigrants from some countries, the more highly educated assimilate more quickly into the labor market. At the same time, there are strong differences among Mexican immigrants who were and were not educated in the United States: Those educated in the United States had nearly twice the number of years of schooling as those immigrants who did not attend U.S. schools, and their earnings were about 30 percent higher.[1]

However, these differences do not necessarily imply that the higher-paid immigrants have better work habits or higher innate productivity. Nor do they necessarily imply that the lower-paid workers are discriminated against. Even after adjusting for differences in years of education, disparities remain in earnings between Mexicans and Central Americans and other immigrant groups. Countries invest differently in the human capital of their citizens, as reflected by the quality of their schools, training programs, and health infrastructure. Before arriving in the United States, immigrants are affected by these investments, so these investments will determine, at least in part, the economic success of the immigrants in the U.S. labor market. In addition, changes in the U.S. wage structure that have favored more-educated workers explain part of the slow growth among some workers. Finally, cultural differences, discrimination, the illegal status of some immigrants, and, perhaps most important, English-language abilities are alternative explanations for the persistent wage gap experienced by Mexican and Central American immigrants, which should be explored in future analyses.

At the same time, the data that are available to researchers to examine immigrant wage growth contain only a limited set of information on workers' skills and abilities. It may be that Mexicans who attended schools of similar quality as those attended by Europeans or Japanese, Koreans, and Chinese achieved similar economic progress. This distinction is important, because if immigrant selection were to be based more heavily on skills (as it is in Canada), then it is possible that government authorities could base their selection on detailed information of the applicant, including his English-language skills and the quality of his education and training.[2] The researcher (using the census data) observes only completed years of education (and self-reported English-language ability); therefore, to the extent that there are differences in the "quality" of workers across countries that are not measured by completed education levels, attempts using the

---

[1]This difference is evaluated at age 35, based on Figure 4.2a.

[2]Of course, evaluating this information would not be costless.

census data to disentangle the reasons for disparities across immigrant groups will be limited.

But whatever the reason for the disparities, a significant number of immigrants in California and the United States currently have very low wages, and the evidence suggests that their wages will not improve substantially throughout their working lives. This evidence, combined with the fact that more-recent immigrants have had lower (age-adjusted) wages relative to earlier immigrants, has substantial ramifications for public-service usage and tax revenues into the future. As well, the trends indicate that the economic and social divisions within communities may be exacerbated. The public and private sectors must explicitly recognize these trends and develop effective policies that will enhance the labor market performance of immigrant groups who fall behind.

EMPIRICAL MODEL, DATA, AND RESULTS

EMPIRICAL MODEL

This appendix describes the empirical models that are the basis of Figures 4.1 and 4.2 and A.1 and A.2. The methods employed are a regression-extension of the cohort analysis discussed in Chapter Three. To illustrate the intuition behind these methods, consider the three censuses examined in the analyses: 1970, 1980, and 1990. Using information on the date of arrival in the United States of each immigrant at each census, we can follow, over time, groups of immigrants who arrived in a given year. For example, we can examine the wages of immigrants who arrived between 1965 and 1969 and who were interviewed in 1970, 1980, and 1990. This general approach has been used in previous studies of assimilation (Baker and Benjamin, 1994; Borjas, 1985, 1992, 1993, 1995; LaLonde and Topel, 1992).

Consider the following model of (log) wages for foreign- and native-born men, for which the 1970, 1980, and 1990 Censuses have been pooled:

$$\log(w) = X'\beta + \alpha I + \sum_{j=1}^{5} \phi_j YSM_j + \sum_{k=1}^{7} \varphi_k C_k$$

$$+ \gamma YEAR80 + \lambda YEAR90 + \varepsilon \qquad (A.1)$$

I is an indicator of being foreign-born (those born abroad of American parents are not considered foreign-born). *YSM* is a set of dummy variables indicating the years since the immigrant arrived in the United States, one each indicating arrival 5–10 years, 10–15 years, 15–20 years, 20–30 years, and 30 or more years prior to the census, which corresponds to the information available in the censuses; those arriving 0–5 years prior to the census are the reference group.[1] C is a set of dummies representing the cohort of arrival of the immigrant, with separate categories for those arriving after 1985, 1980–1984, 1975–1979, 1970–1974, 1960–1964, 1950–1959, and before 1950; those arriving between 1965 and 1969 are the reference group. Variables indicating that the observation is drawn from the 1980 Census (i.e., *YEAR80*) and the 1990 Census (i.e., *YEAR90*) are also included to capture period effects.

The matrix X includes age, education, and interactions between these two variables and other covariates discussed below. Age is specified as a quartic, as recommended by Murphy and Welch (1990).[2] To capture all nonlinearities in the effects of schooling, we specified a step function with indicators for each of the following categories: 0–4 years, 5–8 years, 9 years, 10 years, 11 years, 12 years, 13–15 years, 16 years, and 17 or more years, with 12 years as the reference group. The education question was changed in the 1990 Census; therefore, we translated the 1990 values into the 1980 values. Specifically, those with a General Education Degree are assumed to have 12 years of schooling; those with associate's degrees, 1–3 years of college, or some college are coded as having 13–15 years; those with four years of college or a bachelor's degree are assigned 16

---

[1]The 1990 Census distinguishes between those who immigrated 0–3, 4–5, 6–8, and 9–10 years prior to the census. However, to ensure that differences in wages by years since immigrated are not confounded by differences in wages across years, we do not allow these distinctions. We do, however, control directly for year effects. In addition, previous studies have used a linear version of *YSM*, whereby the midpoint of the category is used as the number of years since migrated. This has the advantage of providing more easily interpreted coefficients, although it imposes additional structure on the data. We prefer the more parsimonious specification.

[2]Murphy and Welch (1990) found that a quadratic in experience tends to overstate the earnings of less-experienced workers. Yuengart (1994) found that the estimates of relative wages of immigrants and natives are sensitive to the specification of age as a quartic versus a quadratic, and that the quartic is preferable.

years; and those with five or more years of college or advanced degrees are assumed to have 17 or more years of schooling.

We allowed the effects of age and education (as specified above) to vary between immigrants and natives, and the effects for both the immigrants and natives to vary among 1970, 1980, and 1990, by interacting age and education separately with *I*, *YEAR80*, and *YEAR90*, and with the products *I*YEAR80* and *I*YEAR90*. To capture differences in the returns to experience at different education levels, we allowed the effects of age (including all higher orders) to vary among those with less than 12 years of schooling, those with 12 years of schooling, and those with more than 12 years of schooling, and these effects varied between immigrants and natives, and among each of the three years. Finally, to test whether the more-skilled immigrants are able to more quickly assimilate into the U.S. labor market, we allowed the effects of the number of years since arrival to vary among those with less than 12 years of schooling, 12 years of schooling, and more than 12 years of schooling.

As is well known, the age, period, and cohort effects cannot each be identified in a linear model.[3] We followed the practice of most previous studies and assumed that the period effects, i.e., γ and λ, are the same for immigrants and natives (Borjas 1995, 1989, 1985; LaLonde and Topel, 1992). All models were examined separately for immigrants from eight groups of countries: Mexico; the United Kingdom (UK) and Canada; Europe; Japan, Korea, and China; the Philippines; Central America; the Middle East and the rest of Asia; and Africa, Caribbean, Oceania, and South America. The share of immigrants in each origin group is listed in Tables 4.7 (the United States as a whole) and A.4 (California). Finally, we estimated each model separately for the United States as a whole and for California.

Although, given available data, the cohort approach is the best technique for determining the extent of wage growth, it has at least three limitations; each limitation concerns changes in the population covered by the census over time:

---

[3]See Borjas (1994) for a discussion of the identification problems associated with this approach in the context of assimilation of immigrants.

- Some immigrants (and natives) leave the country between censuses. Ahmed and Robinson (1994) estimated that 11.3 percent of the 1980 foreign-born population in the United States emigrated by 1990; therefore, the underlying immigrant population has changed. If the individuals who left are the ones who were not assimilating into the labor market, then the estimates from the cohort analysis would overstate the degree of assimilation.

- Some immigrants who came to the United States between the census years may have left the country before being included in a census.

- Although the census attempts to include every individual residing in the United States, some individuals are not counted. Transient populations or individuals who have an incentive to avoid the authorities, such as illegal immigrants, may not all be identified. Moreover, Census Bureau staff (personal communications) believe that the proportion of the population covered was different in each census, and increased significantly between 1970 and 1980; the coverage rates for 1980 and 1990 are thought to be relatively comparable.[4]

To investigate the extent of change in the cohorts both in the nation and in California, we report the number of people in several arrival year–age cohorts and the education distribution of these immigrants. (A recent paper by Ahmed and Robinson [1994] also investigates the

---

[4]Another problem with using census data is that the dates of entry do not always exactly match across censuses. For example, an immigrant interviewed in the 1970 Census who arrived between January 1–April 1 (the day of the census), 1970, would report that the date he arrived was after 1965. Because immigrants were not asked the exact date on which they immigrated, we cannot determine that this immigrant had in fact arrived in the first three months of 1970; therefore, it is assumed that he arrived between 1965 and 1969. We do so because, in 1980, immigrants had to report whether they arrived between 1965–1969 or between 1970–1974. The people who arrived in the first three months of 1970 must be assigned to either the 1965–1969 cohort or the 1970–1974 cohort, and the best choice is to assign them to the former, given that the vast majority arrived during that period. The people who arrived in the first three months of 1970 would then report in 1980 that they arrived between 1970–1974; therefore, the immigrant-year cohort size would change. However, this is presumably a relatively minor effect, with only a small fraction of any five-year immigrant cohort consisting of immigrants who arrived in the first three months of that five-year interval.

change in cohort sizes over time in the United States in order to estimate emigration rates among the foreign-born population. They did not, however, examine whether there were differences in emigration by education.) We also report this information for natives of similar ages. Although education may increase over time, by age 25 most individuals have completed their schooling. Furthermore, we can compare immigrants with natives to see if any change in the education distribution appears to be due to selective emigration rather than to true upgrading in educational attainment.[5]

For the United States, we find that some arrival year–age cohorts *increased* in size between 1970 and 1980, which is consistent with increased coverage by the census (Table A.1). (We report selective cohorts for the United States in Table A.1; full reporting for California is in Table A.2.) The age cohort of 25–29-year-old *natives* also increased between 1970 and 1980. Between 1980 and 1990 the number of immigrants and natives declined, as one would expect from mortality. However, the size of the decline in the cohort was greater for immigrants than for natives. For example, the cohort of those who immigrated in 1965–1969 and who were 25–29 in 1970 decreased by 6.5 percent between 1980 and 1990; the cohort of natives of the same age declined just 2.4 percent. Part of this difference is likely to be due to differential mortality. However, mortality rates for immigrants are not available to let us make comparisons. But given the fairly young ages, the difference is likely to be too large to be completely explained by mortality differentials between immigrants and natives.

Although it appears that some immigrants leave between the censuses, it is not clear that there have been systematic differences in emigration by education. The changes in the education distribution for a given arrival year–age cohort do appear to be upgraded between censuses, but not dramatically (Table A.1). And the upgrading in education that does exist is similar in magnitude to the upgrading taking place among natives. One difference in the change in education distributions between natives and immigrants is that there is a rising share of immigrants in the lowest education group—0–4 years—while this share is always falling for natives. However, in general, the

---

[5]Note that for the comparison with natives to be a meaningful test, educational upgrading for immigrants and natives must be similar.

evidence suggests that differential emigration by education may not be large. Of course, it may be that it is the least-successful immigrants *within* education groups who emigrate, and, if so, the cohort approach overstates true wage growth; this hypothesis cannot be resolved without improved data.

In addition to the complications discussed above for the United States, the analyses for California are hampered by the fact that, between census years, some immigrants moved between states within the United States, which induces changes in the age–immigrant year cohort within California. Unfortunately, there are currently no data that allow us to overcome these difficulties. To gauge the magnitude of this problem, we report the education distributions over time for natives and immigrants in California in Tables A.2b and c and can see that the changes in the education distribution among natives and immigrants are similar. Again, however, there is a slight difference at the lowest end of the education distribution: The number of immigrants with 0–4 years of schooling grows while the number for natives declines. This finding appears to suggest that the least-educated immigrants are most likely to remain in California. However, the change in the proportion falling into this lowest category is on the order of 1–3 percentage points; therefore, it is not likely to substantially influence the estimates of assimilation. However, this evidence is suggestive, not definitive; and until longitudinal data become available it will be difficult to gauge the extent of the bias introduced by nonrandom emigration.

DATA

The data are from the 1-percent sample of the 1970 5-percent county group file, the 1-percent sample of the 1970 state file, the 5-percent 1980-A sample, and the 5-percent 1990-A sample. Both the state and county group files in 1970 were used to increase the number of immigrants in the sample.[6] Men 25–60 years old were selected in order to abstract from differential school leaving and retirement across immigrant groups and natives. Immigrants who did not know their date of entry or country of origin were eliminated, which affected no

---

[6]All descriptive statistics reported in the study use weights to adjust for this fact.

more than 5 percent of immigrants in any census year. The resulting data set consists of 634,219 observations for California and 1,820,923 for the nation. The top-coded reported earnings are used in each year. Borjas (1995) examined the sensitivity of the top-coding and found that the relative wages of immigrants and natives "barely changed" (p. 7) when an imputation scheme was used for top-coded earnings. Therefore, we do not anticipate that top-coding by the census altered our substantive findings.

RESULTS

The parameter estimates from each regression are fully reported in Table A.7 for California and in Table A.8 for all of the United States. At the bottom of each regression table we report the results from four hypothesis tests:

- First, we report whether the effects of age are statistically significantly different for immigrants and natives (in 1970) by conducting an F-test of the joint significance of the four age*immigrant interaction variables—one for each order of the quartic in age.

- Second, we test whether interactions between age and education are statistically significant.

- Third, we test whether the education-age interactions vary between immigrants and natives.

- Fourth, we test whether the interaction between education and age is statistically significant.

Before turning to the multivariate results, it is important to link our analyses with the classic study by Chiswick (1978), who used the 1970 Census to examine the amount that immigrants' relative wages change with the number of years spent in the United States. Chiswick compared the earnings of immigrants who arrived in more-recent periods with those who arrived in earlier periods. This comparison is similar to examining each *row* of Table 4.2. That is, for Europeans in California in 1970, those who entered in 1965–1969 earned 83 percent what natives earned, and those who entered in 1960–1964 earned 110 percent. Relative wages were about the same for those who arrived in 1950–1959, and even higher (122 percent) for those who entered before 1950. These findings suggest that there is strong assimilation among Europeans and that their earnings caught up with and surpassed the earnings of natives within about 10 years. Our more-robust cohort analysis using the 1970, 1980, and 1990 Censuses finds patterns for Europeans similar to those of Chiswick.

However, the conclusions drawn from our cohort approach and Chiswick's approach are diametrically opposed for immigrants from Mexico. If only a single cross section were used, it would appear that the relative earnings of immigrants improved over time. For example, consider the group of Mexican immigrants who entered the United States in the same years as the Europeans discussed in the preceding paragraph. The relative earnings for Mexicans who entered in 1965–1969 and who were 25–34 years old in 1970 were 54 percent. The relative wages were higher for immigrants who arrived in earlier cohorts: 68, 72, and 80 percent for those arriving in 1960–1965, 1950–1959, and 1950 or before, respectively. However, the cohort approach demonstrates that relative wages actually *declined*. For those who were 25–34 years old in 1970 and arrived between 1965 and 1969, relative earnings declined from 54 percent in 1970 to 49 percent in 1990.

In sum, this discussion highlights the importance of using cohort methods instead of a single cross section of data to draw conclusions regarding economic progress.

Calculation of Predicted Age-Earnings Profile

The predicted age-earnings profiles displayed in Figures 4.1 and 4.2 and A.1 and A.2 are based on the regressions in Tables A.7 and A.8. For each country, we calculated the predicted earnings, assuming that immigrants arrived in the United States at age 25 (i.e., years in the United States is equal to zero when age is equal to 25). As the immigrant ages five years, his earnings increase from the effect of experience (i.e., the coefficients on A and all its interactions) and the effect of assimilation (i.e., the coefficients on YSM and its interaction with education). The earnings profile is then traced by adding the age and assimilation effects for the corresponding points in the life profile: i.e., age 30 and duration in the United States of 5–10 years, age 35 and duration in the United States of 10–15 years, age 40 and duration in the United States of 15–20 years, and age 50 and duration in the United States of 20–30 years.[7]

The profiles are evaluated at the mean levels of education for each immigrant group and for natives. Specifically, the weight given to each education coefficient corresponds to the proportion of each origin group falling into the given education category. For example, if 15 percent of Mexicans have 5–8 years of schooling, that coefficient would receive a weight of .15 in calculating predicted earnings. Unless stated otherwise, the effects on the entry cohort, C, are also evaluated at the mean levels for each origin group.

The effects of age and education are allowed to vary over time. In calculating the predicted earnings, we used a weighted average of the coefficients for each year on these variables, where the weights are the shares of all workers in the three-year merged data set that were observed in the respective year.

To identify the model, we assumed the year effects to be the same for immigrants and natives. Therefore, the estimated age-earnings profile for natives will depend on the origin group–specific regression equation that is used. We used the regression that merges natives with Mexican immigrants to generate the earnings profile for natives, although the native profiles are very similar when the regressions representing the other origin groups are used.

Estimated Effect of Assimilation

The assimilation effect is represented by the coefficients on the indicators for the years since arrived in the United States, i.e., ϕ_j, which is the log approximation of the percentage differences.[8] For example, referring to Table A.4 for Mexicans in California, the assimilation effect for someone with 12 years of schooling who has been in the United States 5–10 years is 16.9 percent. The marginal effect of being in the United States an additional five years is 0.8 percent (=17.7 – 16.9). The specification allows the assimilation effect to vary among

---

[7]Somewhat similar methods were used by LaLonde and Topel (1992) and Borjas (1995) to generate earnings profiles.

[8]In only a few instances are the coefficients large enough to make the log approximation somewhat imprecise.

those with less than 12 years of schooling, exactly 12 years of schooling, and more than 12 years of schooling. The total assimilation effect for each group is reported in Table A.4 and Table 4.5 for California and the nation, respectively.

We conducted a variety of tests to examine the statistical significance of the assimilation effects, reported in Tables A.5 and A.6. For each (classical) test, we report the P-value.

- First, we tested whether the effect of assimilation up to the given number of years is statistically significantly different from zero for each education level.

- We then tested whether the marginal effect of assimilation is significant. That is, is the effect of assimilation through 10–15 years different from the assimilation effect through 5–10 years? This test was conducted for each education level.

- Third, we reported whether the assimilation effect is different across education levels, for each individual assimilation and education level, and for all levels as a group. For example, we tested whether the effects of being in the United States 10–15 years is the same for someone with less than 12 years of schooling and for someone with more than 12 years of schooling.

- We also tested, for each number of years of assimilation, whether the assimilation is different between those with 12 years and less than 12 years of schooling, and between those with 12 years and more than 12 years of schooling. We then tested whether all the interactions between education and years since immigrated are jointly zero.

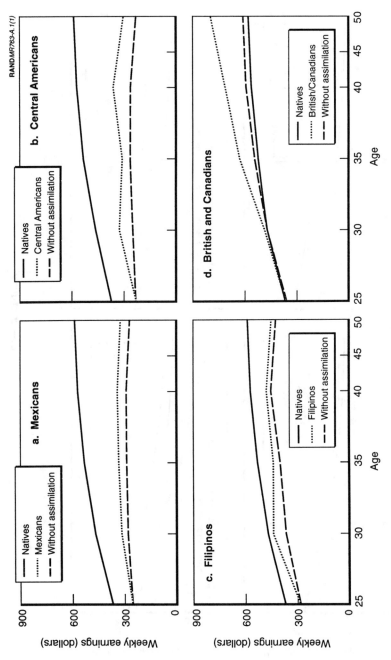

Figures A.1—Earnings Profiles of Immigrants in the United States (With and Without Assimilation Effects)

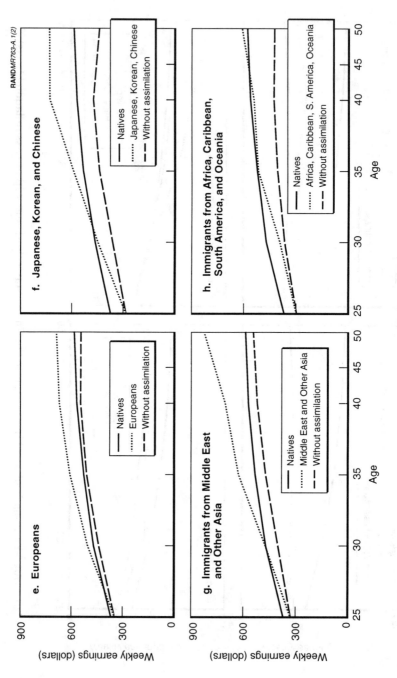

Figures A.1—continued

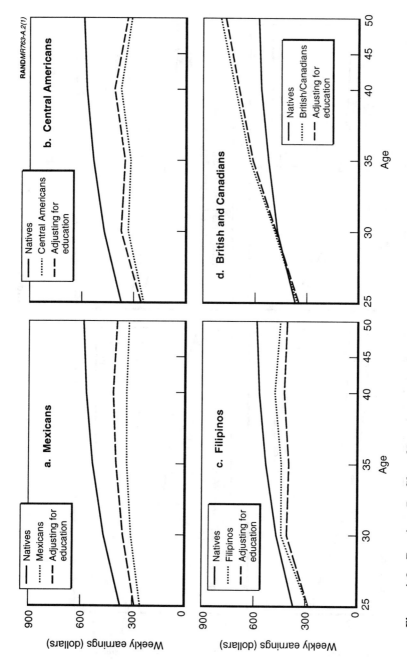

Figure A.2—Earnings Profiles of Immigrants in the United States (With and Without Education Adjustment)

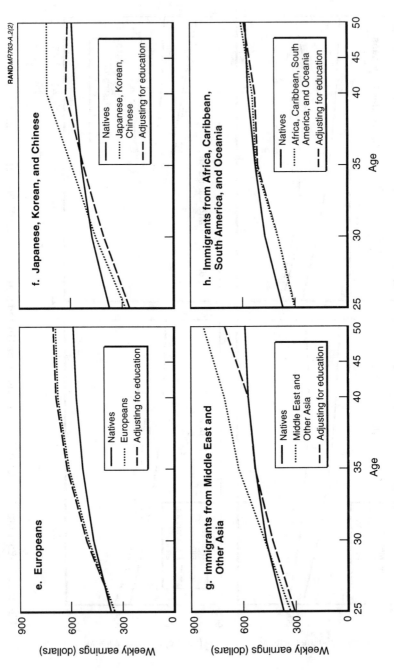

Figure A.2—continued

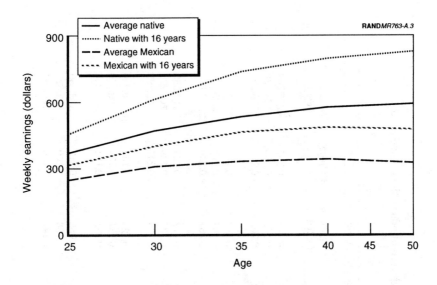

Figure A.3—Earnings Profiles of Mexicans and Natives with Various Levels of Education (With and Without Education Adjustments), United States

Table A.1

Distribution of Education for Arrival Year–Age Cohorts, All Individuals in the United States (1970–1990)

Arrival Year/ Age in Census Year/ Census	0–4 Years	5–8 Years	9–11 Years	12 Years	Some College	College Degree	Number of People
1965–1969/25–29 in 1970							
1970	0.065	0.163	0.120	0.236	0.148	0.267	257,200
1980	0.074	0.164	0.103	0.246	0.163	0.250	274,120
1990	0.081	0.121	0.070	0.246	0.205	0.278	256,251
Born U.S./25–29 in 1970							
1970	0.015	0.068	0.173	0.425	0.152	0.167	12,774,850
1980	0.010	0.056	0.132	0.408	0.184	0.210	12,895,640
1990	0.010	0.039	0.099	0.350	0.267	0.235	12,563,054
1965–1969/30–34 in 1970							
1970	0.083	0.233	0.119	0.200	0.112	0.254	203,550
1980	0.091	0.214	0.103	0.239	0.125	0.228	200,220
1990	0.097	0.167	0.069	0.247	0.174	0.247	189,799
Born U.S./30–34 in 1970							
1970	0.018	0.094	0.196	0.422	0.126	0.145	10,770,950
1980	0.015	0.078	0.155	0.419	0.161	0.173	10,603,200
1990	0.014	0.058	0.124	0.380	0.233	0.191	10,311,358
1965–1969/35–39 in 1970							
1970	0.112	0.270	0.124	0.193	0.089	0.212	133,850
1980	0.115	0.246	0.097	0.235	0.108	0.200	142,820
1990	0.147	0.189	0.085	0.254	0.147	0.178	124,254

Proportion of Age and Entry Cohort

Table A.1—continued

Arrival Year/ Age in Census Year/ Census	Proportion of Age and Entry Cohort						
	0–4 Years	5–8 Years	9–11 Years	12 Years	Some College	College Degree	Number of People
Born U.S./35–39 in 1970							
1970	0.024	0.125	0.200	0.398	0.115	0.138	10,394,400
1980	0.021	0.109	0.167	0.401	0.143	0.158	10,184,880
1990	0.022	0.086	0.136	0.379	0.204	0.173	9,543,452
1975–1979/25–29 in 1980							
1980	0.082	0.153	0.097	0.215	0.196	0.257	514,240
1990	0.113	0.139	0.075	0.205	0.200	0.268	448,893
Born U.S./25–29 in 1980							
1980	0.007	0.028	0.106	0.400	0.236	0.223	18,100,380
1990	0.006	0.017	0.066	0.320	0.325	0.266	17,967,059
1975–1979/30–34 in 1980							
1980	0.084	0.141	0.091	0.216	0.157	0.311	357,320
1990	0.131	0.121	0.071	0.224	0.180	0.273	301,350
Born U.S./30–34 in 1980							
1980	0.008	0.039	0.101	0.381	0.224	0.247	16,340,360
1990	0.008	0.025	0.071	0.313	0.306	0.278	15,871,273
1975–1979/35–39 in 1980							
1980	0.105	0.169	0.092	0.216	0.142	0.276	209,580
1990	0.145	0.139	0.070	0.246	0.171	0.230	179,076
Born U.S./35–39 in 1980							
1980	0.010	0.056	0.132	0.408	0.184	0.210	12,895,640
1990	0.010	0.039	0.099	0.350	0.267	0.235	12,563,054

Table A.2

Education Distribution of Each Cohort

a. Immigrants and Natives in California (1970–1990)

Year Immigrated/ Age in Census Year/ Census	Number of Immigrants	Education Distribution (percent in each category)					
		0–4 Years	5–8 Years	9–11 Years	12 Years	Some College	College Degree
1975–1979							
20–24 in 1970							
1970							
1980	111,620	13.4	18.2	9.3	18.5	14.9	25.7
1990	106,285	15.7	15.2	5.5	18.7	17.9	27.0
25–29 in 1970							
1970							
1980	66,080	15.9	20.4	8.4	19.2	12.7	23.2
1990	62,946	18.6	14.9	6.7	19.9	17.3	22.6
30–34 in 1970							
1970							
1980	43,540	18.2	21.7	8.8	19.6	11.9	19.8
1990	44,437	20.6	15.1	6.4	19.9	17.2	20.8
35–39 in 1970							
1970							
1980	32,160	19.6	20.3	10.8	19.9	11.3	18.2
1990	28,635	22.5	15.2	6.6	21.1	15.0	19.7
40–44 in 1970							
1970							
1980	26,380	24.6	22.9	11.6	17.3	10.0	13.6
1990	22,084	22.8	15.7	6.4	21.3	13.0	17.9

Table A.2a—continued

Year Immigrated/ Age in Census Year/ Census	Number of Immigrants	Education Distribution (percent in each category)						
		0–4 Years	5–8 Years	9–11 Years	12 Years	Some College	College Degree
1975–1979							
45–49 in 1970							
1970	15,900	24.8	22.9	12.6	21.1	7.6	11.0
1980	14,520	22.7	22.7	10.3	18.3	10.9	15.0
1990							
50–54 in 1970							
1970	9750	23.6	30.8	11.3	20.0	7.2	7.2
1980	9480	25.5	23.8	9.3	20.0	7.6	13.7
1990							
55–59 in 1970							
1970	9850	29.4	30.9	8.6	16.8	3.6	10.7
1980							
1990							
60–64 in 1970							
1970	5950	27.7	34.5	10.1	15.1	8.4	4.2
1980							
1990							

Table A.2a—continued

Year Immigrated/ Age in Census Year/ Census	Number of Immigrants	Education Distribution (percent in each category)						
		0–4 Years	5–8 Years	9–11 Years	12 Years	Some College	College Degree
1970–1974								
20–24 in 1970								
1970								
1980	109,620	13.9	23.9	9.4	16.4	14.4	21.8
1990	111,618	16.7	18.4	7.1	17.2	17.3	23.4
25–29 in 1970								
1970								
1980	65,220	16.4	23.7	8.1	15.8	12.3	23.7
1990	69,569	18.5	17.9	6.0	17.2	15.3	25.1
30–34 in 1970								
1970								
1980	41,320	18.1	23.2	8.2	16.8	11.4	22.3
1990	41,159	23.1	15.8	5.9	18.4	13.9	23.0
35–39 in 1970								
1970								
1980	24,920	24.1	23.4	9.9	16.9	8.8	17.0
1990	24,816	25.1	17.2	6.7	19.0	13.0	19.1
40–44 in 1970								
1970								
1980	18,100	23.9	24.2	9.8	18.3	8.6	15.1
1990	16,673	24.9	18.0	8.1	21.2	11.4	16.4

Table A.2a—continued

Year Immigrated/ Age in Census Year/ Census	Number of Immigrants	Education Distribution (percent in each category)					
		0–4 Years	5–8 Years	9–11 Years	12 Years	Some College	College Degree
1970–1974							
45–49 in 1970							
1970							
1980	12,580	25.3	24.9	7.6	19.4	9.5	13.2
1990							
50–54 in 1970							
1970							
1980	9260	27.9	25.3	8.9	20.9	8.0	9.1
1990							
55–59 in 1970							
1970							
1980							
1990							
60–64 in 1970							
1970							
1980							
1990							

Table A.2a—continued

Year Immigrated/ Age in Census Year/ Census	Number of Immigrants	Education Distribution (percent in each category)					
		0–4 Years	5–8 Years	9–11 Years	12 Years	Some College	College Degree
1965–1969							
20–24 in 1970							
1970	54,750	9.5	21.1	15.5	23.7	22.2	7.9
1980	73,360	11.7	23.9	10.2	19.1	18.0	17.1
1990	74,504	13.3	18.1	8.1	20.6	21.6	18.3
25–29 in 1970							
1970	56,500	10.1	18.8	10.9	23.5	17.4	19.2
1980	70,720	11.0	19.4	8.7	19.6	17.4	23.9
1990	69,861	13.2	15.7	7.0	19.2	21.4	23.6
30–34 in 1970							
1970	40,950	11.7	20.5	11.2	19.4	13.1	24.1
1980	46,920	12.2	21.7	8.4	21.5	12.6	23.6
1990	46,324	13.6	14.5	5.9	21.6	19.2	25.3
35–39 in 1970							
1970	28,750	14.4	22.3	11.1	21.0	10.4	20.7
1980	29,920	15.4	22.7	9.7	21.7	10.6	19.9
1990	28,544	18.4	15.9	7.1	23.2	17.8	17.8
40–44 in 1970							
1970	19,950	19.3	25.3	12.0	21.0	9.8	12.5
1980	21,920	19.3	23.8	8.9	20.7	11.6	15.7
1990	18,889	21.5	18.4	7.7	21.9	15.0	15.4

Table A.2a—continued

Year Immigrated/ Age in Census Year/ Census	Number of Immigrants	Education Distribution (percent in each category)					
		0–4 Years	5–8 Years	9–11 Years	12 Years	Some College	College Degree
1965–1969							
45–49 in 1970							
1970	15,900	24.8	22.9	12.6	21.1	7.6	11.0
1980	14,520	22.7	22.7	10.3	18.3	10.9	15.0
1990							
50–54 in 1970							
1970	9750	23.6	30.8	11.3	20.0	7.2	7.2
1980	9480	25.5	23.8	9.3	20.0	7.6	13.7
1990							
55–59 in 1970							
1970	9850	29.4	30.9	8.6	16.8	3.6	10.7
1980							
1990							
60–64 in 1970							
1970	5950	27.7	34.5	10.1	15.1	8.4	4.2
1980							
1990							

Table A.2

Education Distribution of Each Cohort
b. Immigrants in California (1970–1990)

Year Immigrated/ Age in Census Year/ Census	Number of Immigrants	Education Distribution (percent in each category)					
		0–4 Years	5–8 Years	9–11 Years	12 Years	Some College	College Degree
1960–1964							
20–24 in 1970							
1970	26,850	6.3	18.3	14.9	32.8	21.9	5.8
1980	32,580	6.6	15.8	11.5	26.1	24.5	15.5
1990	31,315	8.3	13.4	9.2	23.2	27.4	18.4
25–29 in 1970							
1970	41,000	10.9	21.5	11.1	27.7	18.7	10.0
1980	48,980	9.3	19.1	10.7	24.1	19.1	17.8
1990	49,635	12.4	13.9	7.0	22.9	25.5	18.3
30–34 in 1970							
1970	48,900	7.9	23.0	14.2	24.6	17.9	12.3
1980	55,620	10.5	18.4	10.3	24.8	17.6	18.5
1990	55,618	10.5	13.4	6.7	25.2	25.8	18.5
35–39 in 1970							
1970	36,050	12.2	21.6	14.6	26.8	14.4	10.4
1980	39,560	14.6	18.3	11.2	25.0	16.0	15.0
1990	37,505	14.3	15.4	7.1	26.5	21.6	15.2
40–44 in 1970							
1970	26,950	15.4	24.7	14.7	21.7	14.1	9.5
1980	27,440	14.4	20.2	12.2	24.3	16.3	12.7
1990	23,973	18.3	14.6	8.1	26.0	20.6	12.5

Table A.2b—continued

Year Immigrated/ Age in Census Year/ Census	Number of Immigrants	Education Distribution (percent in each category)						
		0–4 Years	5–8 Years	9–11 Years	12 Years	Some College	College Degree
1960–1964								
45–49 in 1970								
1970	17,950	17.6	18.7	15.3	27.3	12.8	8.4
1980	18,340	16.6	20.9	10.4	26.5	13.2	12.4
1990								
50–54 in 1970								
1970	10,350	22.2	26.6	13.5	18.8	10.6	8.2
1980	10,560	16.7	23.3	12.3	24.8	12.3	10.6
1990								
55–59 in 1970								
1970	9650	22.3	25.4	13.0	22.3	10.4	6.8
1980								
1990								
60–64 in 1970								
1970	6650	24.1	23.3	11.3	20.3	10.5	10.5
1980								
1990								

Table A.2b—continued

Year Immigrated/ Age in Census Year/ Census	Number of Immigrants	Education Distribution (percent in each category)					
		0–4 Years	5–8 Years	9–11 Years	12 Years	Some College	College Degree
1950–1959							
20–24 in 1970							
1970	31,950	2.0	6.7	11.4	36.2	37.4	6.3
1980	39,000	1.6	4.0	6.8	29.8	21.4	26.5
1990	35,414	1.4	2.5	5.3	20.8	39.6	30.5
25–29 in 1970							
1970	31,950	5.5	14.7	16.6	31.5	19.6	13.2
1980	33,220	4.8	12.3	12.5	28.6	24.1	17.6
1990	30,118	5.7	10.2	8.0	25.2	29.7	21.3
30–34 in 1970							
1970	43,050	9.2	18.4	13.5	27.8	17.4	13.8
1980	51,340	7.7	17.6	11.5	28.0	19.8	15.4
1990	46,924	9.4	12.1	8.1	26.5	27.4	16.5
35–39 in 1970							
1970	58,900	9.9	21.5	12.6	28.6	16.2	11.2
1980	62,940	9.7	16.0	10.4	29.6	19.5	14.9
1990	61,653	11.6	13.6	7.5	28.3	23.7	15.3
40–44 in 1970							
1970	53,750	11.1	19.5	14.9	26.6	15.2	12.7
1980	58,780	11.1	17.5	11.2	26.8	19.0	14.4
1990	53,222	12.3	12.6	8.0	28.6	23.6	15.0

Table A.2b—continued

Year Immigrated/ Age in Census Year/ Census	Number of Immigrants	Education Distribution (percent in each category)					
		0-4 Years	5-8 Years	9-11 Years	12 Years	Some College	College Degree
1950–1959							
45-49 in 1970							
1970	42,250	12.9	22.5	12.3	26.9	14.4	10.9
1980	43,120	13.2	19.8	10.5	25.2	17.3	14.1
1990							
50-54 in 1970							
1970	24,700	11.5	26.3	11.9	27.7	10.9	11.5
1980	26,060	14.0	18.9	12.9	26.5	14.6	12.9
1990							
55-59 in 1970							
1970	20,550	18.0	29.2	12.7	22.6	10.0	7.5
1980							
1990							
60-64 in 1970							
1970	11,950	18.0	26.8	14.3	27.2	5.0	8.8
1980							
1990							

Table A.2

Education Distribution of Each Cohort
c. Natives in California (1970–1990)

Age in Census Year/Census	Number of Immigrants	Education Distribution (percent in each category)						
		0–4 Years	5–8 Years	9–11 Years	12 Years	Some College	College Degree
20–24 in 1970								
1970	1,577,300	0.9	2.2	13.2	39.9	34.4	9.3
1980	1,651,660	0.7	1.7	7.6	30.3	31.7	28.2
1990	1,615,398	0.6	1.0	4.2	21.7	39.5	33.0
25–29 in 1970								
1970	1,301,250	0.9	3.3	14.9	37.9	23.9	19.1
1980	1,259,640	0.7	2.5	9.7	33.1	27.6	26.4
1990	1,236,824	0.7	1.6	6.1	25.0	36.2	30.4
30–34 in 1970								
1970	1,059,850	1.1	4.7	16.9	38.8	20.4	18.1
1980	1,015,400	1.0	3.7	12.1	34.9	25.1	23.2
1990	986,123	0.9	2.5	8.3	28.5	33.4	26.4
35–39 in 1970								
1970	998,100	1.5	6.9	17.6	37.6	18.9	17.6
1980	938,980	1.3	5.6	12.9	35.4	23.4	21.3
1990	868,827	1.5	4.2	9.7	30.9	29.7	24.0
40–44 in 1970								
1970	1,077,450	2.1	9.6	19.3	35.9	16.9	16.3
1980	1,011,720	2.1	7.8	15.6	35.8	20.3	18.6
1990	880,931	2.0	5.9	12.2	32.6	26.9	20.4

Table A.2c—continued

Age in Census Year/Census	Number of Immigrants	Education Distribution (percent in each category)						
		0–4 Years	5–8 Years	9–11 Years	12 Years	Some College	College Degree
45–49 in 1970							
1970	1,104,850	2.2	10.4	18.0	38.2	17.4	13.9
1980	1,039,200	2.1	9.0	14.8	38.1	19.8	16.2
1990							
50–54 in 1970							
1970	988,700	2.0	13.5	19.2	37.2	16.2	12.0
1980	868,460	2.3	12.3	16.2	37.7	18.0	13.8
1990							
55–59 in 1970							
1970	832,150	3.0	18.2	20.9	32.7	14.4	10.9
1980							
1990							
60–64 in 1970							
1970	660,650	3.9	24.1	21.7	26.8	13.4	10.0
1980							
1990							

Table A.3

Relative Median Earnings of Men in California and the Nation, by Country of Origin (1970–1990)

Country of Origin	California				United States			
	1970	1980	1990		1970	1980	1990	
Mexico	60	55	47		69	61	53	
Japan, Korea, China	70	80	88		81	88	100	
Central America	74	52	45		81	61	52	
Philippines	62	70	73		72	77	83	
Europe	100	103	105		104	106	112	
Middle East, Other Asia	90	87	91		104	98	104	
Africa, Caribbean, South America, Oceania	79	80	81		81	79	80	
Indochina/Vietnam	—	60	64		—	66	70	
UK, Canada	104	110	117		116	118	126	

Table A.4

Percentage[a] Gain in Weekly Earnings Relative to Being in the United States Less Than Five Years, by Country of Origin and Years of Schooling, in California

Percentage Gain

Number of Years in U.S.	Mexico (39.1%)[b] Years of Education			UK/Canada (7.3%)[b] Years of Education		
	Less than 12	12 Years	More than 12	Less than 12	12 Years	More than 12
5–10	12.7	16.9	14.0	5.7	-0.9	6.1
10–15	13.7	17.7	20.8	17.3	17.2	25.0
15–20	14.7	22.4	24.7	29.6	20.3	29.0
20–30	15.3	17.8	26.2	35.0	31.7	35.1
30 or more	12.6	20.6	32.3	38.7	48.1	50.1

Percentage Gain

Number of Years in U.S.	Europe (11.6%)[b] Years of Education			Japan/Korea/China (10.1%)[b] Years of Education		
	Less than 12	12 Years	More than 12	Less than 12	12 Years	More than 12
5–10	15.1	17.2	5.3	25.9	24.8	21.8
10–15	24.0	19.4	24.4	45.5	39.5	36.4
15–20	16.5	15.0	21.8	56.6	45.5	48.8
20–30	26.7	22.3	26.6	64.7	57.3	65.8
30 or more	25.4	22.0	27.0	83.3	81.8	93.4

Table A.4—continued

Percentage Gain

Number of Years in U.S.	Philippines (7.2%)[b]			Middle East, Other Asia (7.5%)[b]		
	Years of Education			Years of Education		
	Less than 12	12 Years	More than 12	Less than 12	12 Years	More than 12
5–10	19.8	19.8	26.2	20.4	12.7	15.4
10–15	-0.7	10.2	16.8	42.1	7.8	25.2
15–20	10.1	10.0	25.4	21.5	12.7	28.2
20–30	1.3	9.1	17.1	45.9	41.6	37.5
30 or more	-13.0	-3.2	3.3	24.2	29.8	49.5

Percentage Gain

Number of Years in U.S.	Central America (6.4%)[b]			Africa, Caribbean, South America, Oceania (7.4%)[b]		
	Years of Education			Years of Education		
	Less than 12	12 Years	More than 12	Less than 12	12 Years	More than 12
5–10	27.9	28.2	37.5	10.1	6.5	2.8
10–15	28.6	26.9	34.3	40.5	41.9	42.7
15–20	45.2	47.1	57.1	44.1	33.1	36.0
20–30	52.4	48.6	50.3	74.2	53.0	57.1
30 or more	48.3	58.6	71.1	71.2	78.4	82.5

[a]Percent difference is based on the log approximation.
[b]Number in parentheses is the percentage of immigrants who are from the given country of origin.

Table A.5

P-Values from F-Tests of Restrictions on Differences in Assimilation Among Education Groups, in California

| | Mexico | | | | United Kingdom/Canada | | | |
| | Years of Schooling | | | | Years of Schooling | | | |
Restriction	<12	12	>12	All	<12	12	>12	All
0–5 yrs=5–10 yrs	.0001	.0001	.0006		.5297	.9103	.3956	
5–10 yrs=10–15 yrs	.8220	.8667	.1872		.2363	.0303	.0131	
10–15 yrs=15–20 yrs	.7031	.1706	.3086		.1434	.6389	.4698	
15–20 yrs=20–30 yrs	.8837	.2997	.7427		.5041	.0658	.2568	
20–30 yrs=30 or more yrs	.5055	.5724	.2186		.6004	.0032	.0026	
5–10 yrs*education=0	.1033	.0001	.4075		.4613	.9103	.2925	
10–15 yrs*education=0	.1291	.0001	.4098		.9908	.0182	.2286	
15–20 yrs*education=0	.0058	.0001	.5493		.2819	.0101	.1501	
20–30 yrs*education=0	.3478	.0163	.0129		.6319	.0008	.4522	
30+ yrs*education=0	.0403	.0590	.0084		.2097	.0001	.6781	
All length of stay*education interactions=0	.0078		.0078	.0001	.3676		.6953	.6518
5–10 for <12=5–10 for >12				.6851				.9681
10–15 for <12=10–15 for >12				.0238				.3764
15–20 for <12=15–20 for >12				.0021				.9379
20–30 for <12=20–30 for >12				.0003				.9958
30+ for <12=30+ for >12				.0001				.1436

Table A.5—continued

	P-Value							
	Europe				Japan, Korea, China			
	Years of Schooling				Years of Schooling			
Restriction	<12	12	>12	All	<12	12	>12	All
0–5 yrs=5–10 yrs	.0194	.0076	.3594		.0004	.0004	.0006	
5–10 yrs=10–15 yrs	.1789	.7521	.0021		.0527	.1310	.0980	
10–15 yrs=15–20 yrs	.1439	.4017	.5464		.1867	.4194	.0279	
15–20 yrs=20–30 yrs	.0632	.1649	.2942		.4374	.2060	.0296	
20–30 yrs=30 or more yrs	.7961	.9493	.9220		.0439	.0065	.0005	
5–10 yrs*education=0	.7514	.0076	.0325		.8553	.0004	.4652	
10–15 yrs*education=0	.4576	.0012	.3399		.3880	.0001	.5234	
15–20 yrs*education=0	.8050	.0261	.1883		.1617	.0001	.5521	
20–30 yrs*education=0	.4189	.0065	.2942		.2747	.0001	.0610	
30+ yrs*education=0	.5802	.0457	.2638		.8485	.0001	.0322	
All length of stay*education interactions=0	.8950		.0212	.1208	.6887		.0606	.1164
5–10 for < 12=5–10 for > 12				.1164				.4160
10–15 for < 12=10–15 for > 12				.9548				.1305
15–20 for < 12=15–20 for > 12				.3791				.2594
20–30 for < 12=20–30 for > 12				.9822				.8571
30+ for < 12=30+ for > 12				.7868				.1613

Table A.5—continued

	P-Value							
	Philippines				Middle East, Other Asia			
	Years of Schooling				Years of Schooling			
Restriction	<12	12	>12	All	<12	12	>12	All
0–5 yrs=5–10 yrs	.0453	.0226	.0007		.0205	.1137	.0319	
5–10 yrs=10–15 yrs	.1610	.4645	.4495		.1318	.7243	.4534	
10–15 yrs=15–20 yrs	.3171	.9807	.2197		.0519	.5693	.6363	
15–20 yrs=20–30 yrs	.5475	.9432	.4804		.1278	.0343	.4465	
20–30 yrs=30 or more yrs	.2610	.3036	.2311		.2013	.3855	.3432	
5–10 yrs*education=0	.9975	.0226	.2130		.2651	.1137	.5755	
10–15 yrs*education=0	.2055	.3786	.2130		.0001	.5300	.0014	
15–20 yrs*education=0	.9960	.4586	.0086		.3672	.3648	.0108	
20–30 yrs*education=0	.3185	.6706	.0962		.6308	.0727	.4508	
30+ yrs*education=0	.2587	.9164	.2914		.5765	.3775	.0033	
All length of stay*education interactions=0	.6243		.1521	.1701	.0010		.0002	.0001
5–10 for < 12=5–10 for > 12				.3823				.4275
10–15 for < 12=10–15 for > 12				.0279				.0116
15–20 for < 12=15–20 for > 12				.0923				.4419
20–30 for < 12=20–30 for > 12				.0446				.3398
30+ for < 12=30+ for > 12				.0801				.0227

Table A.5—continued

				P-Value				
	Central America				Africa, Caribb., S. Amer., Oceania			
	Years of Schooling				Years of Schooling			
Restriction	<12	12	>12	All	<12	12	>12	All
0–5 yrs=5–10 yrs	.0033	.0047	.0002		.1530	.3367	.6547	
5–10 yrs=10–15 yrs	.9640	.9367	.8482		.0091	.0018	.0002	
10–15 yrs=15–20 yrs	.0740	.0320	.0159		.6227	.1704	.2049	
15–20 yrs=20–30 yrs	.6572	.9259	.6531		.0095	.0607	.0336	
20–30 yrs=30 or more yrs	.8149	.5401	.1944		.8219	.0276	.0176	
5–10 yrs*education=0	.9599	.0047	.0907		.5686	.3367	.4537	
10–15 yrs*education=0	.7424	.0702	.2442		.8370	.0001	.8888	
15–20 yrs*education=0	.8041	.0064	.1580		.1309	.0034	.5849	
20–30 yrs*education=0	.5751	.0868	.7574		.0018	.0053	.3649	
30+ yrs*education=0	.2867	.1641	.0643		.4176	.0059	.4870	
All length of stay*education interactions=0	.8730		.2679	.3409	.0145		.7191	.0638
5–10 for < 12=5–10 for > 12				.0534				.2141
10–15 for < 12=10–15 for > 12				.3392				.2354
15–20 for < 12=15–20 for > 12				.1089				.0106
20–30 for < 12=20–30 for > 12				.7550				.0638
30+ for < 12=30+ for > 12				.0286				.0001

Table A.6

P-Values from F-Tests of Restrictions on Differences in Assimilation Among Education Groups, for the Nation

	P-Value							
	Mexico				UK/Canada			
	Years of Schooling				Years of Schooling			
Restriction	<12	12	>12	All	<12	12	>12	All
0–5 yrs=5–10 yrs	.0001	.0001	.0031		.0663	.9215	.3939	
5–10 yrs=10–15 yrs	.5975	.7429	.1226		.0167	.0878	.1995	
10–15 yrs=15–20 yrs	.9272	.1993	.2689		.4773	.4856	.1832	
15–20 yrs=20–30 yrs	.3965	.3798	.9760		.1244	.0159	.1212	
20–30 yrs=30 or more yrs	.5258	.2768	.2846		.5616	.1657	.0308	
5–10 yrs*education=0	.4462	.0001	.2601		.0759	.9215	.4342	
10–15 yrs*education=0	.6199	.0001	.5195		.0065	.0314	.8912	
15–20 yrs*education=0	.0318	.0001	.5553		.0032	.0108	.5233	
20–30 yrs*education=0	.7209	.0097	.0470		.0025	.0001	.5687	
30+ yrs*education=0	.0615	.0232	.1001		.1500	.0002	.8648	
All length of stay/education interactions=0	.0808		.0682	.0031	.0086		.8563	.0346
5–10 for < 12=5–10 for > 12				.5099				.2678
10–15 for < 12=10–15 for > 12				.2450				.0082
15–20 for < 12=15–20 for > 12				.0122				.0169
20–30 for < 12=20–30 for > 12				.0798				.0010
30+ yrs*education=0				.0009				.2324

Table A.6—continued

	P-Value							
	Europe				Japan, Korea, China			
	Years of Schooling				Years of Schooling			
Restriction	<12	12	>12	All	<12	12	>12	All
0–5 yrs=5–10 yrs	.0001	.0001	.0181		.0001	.0006	.0001	
5–10 yrs=10–15 yrs	.0303	.8237	.0370		.1868	.2625	.1860	
10–15 yrs=15–20 yrs	.4463	.6836	.5364		.0588	.1832	.0075	
15–20 yrs=20–30 yrs	.0608	.9409	.5219		.6656	.3932	.1744	
20–30 yrs=30 or more yrs	.0120	.5799	.5933		.0134	.0012	.0046	
5–10 yrs*education=0	.6088	.0001	.0232		.1814	.0006	.6792	
10–15 yrs*education=0	.1808	.0001	.7122		.1373	.0001	.6056	
15–20 yrs*education=0	.1179	.0001	.8063		.0346	.0001	.1629	
20–30 yrs*education=0	.0003	.0001	.6447		.0608	.0002	.0124	
30+ yrs*education=0	.0564	.0036	.6227		.3399	.0001	.3171	
All length of stay/education interactions=0	.0023		.1377	.0087	.1550		.1664	.2012
5–10 for < 12=5–10 for > 12				.0933				.2559
10–15 for < 12=10–15 for > 12				.0735				.2098
15–20 for < 12=15–20 for > 12				.0670				.2428
20–30 for < 12=20–30 for > 12				.0012				.8428
30+ yrs*education=0				.1416				.8629

Table A.6—continued

	P-Value							
	Philippines				Middle East, Other Asia			
	Years of Schooling				Years of Schooling			
Restriction	<12	12	>12	All	<12	12	>12	All
0–5 yrs=5–10 yrs	.0009	.0138	.0002		.0004	.0134	.0014	.0002
5–10 yrs=10–15 yrs	.1084	.4009	.4620		.0965	.9500	.1708	.1710
10–15 yrs=15–20 yrs	.1579	.6074	.3442		.1744	.9549	.5016	.0291
15–20 yrs=20–30 yrs	.6870	.8892	.3782		.0694	.0162	.2631	.7113
20–30 yrs=30 or more yrs	.1853	.2413	.0431		.9118	.6549	.4600	.1699
5–10 yrs*education=0	.1459	.0138	.1664		.1087	.0134	.6301	.6428
10–15 yrs*education=0	.8862	.3554	.0847		.0001	.0824	.0011	
15–20 yrs*education=0	.0363	.6333	.0006		.0324	.1201	.0005	
20–30 yrs*education=0	.1440	.7003	.0593		.0639	.0161	.4586	
30+ yrs*education=0	.1998	.8616	.8034		.1524	.0656	.2221	
All length of stay/education interactions=0	.1249		.0174	.0293	.0005		.0010	.0002
5–10 for < 12=5–10 for > 12				.6199				.1710
10–15 for < 12=10–15 for > 12				.1660				.0291
15–20 for < 12=15–20 for > 12				.7837				.7113
20–30 for < 12=20–30 for > 12				.7786				.1699
30+ yrs*education=0				.2033				.6428

Table A.6—continued

| | Central America | | | | Africa, Caribb., S. Amer., Oceania | | | |
| | Years of Schooling | | | | Years of Schooling | | | |
Restriction	<12	12	>12	All	<12	12	>12	All
0–5 yrs=5–10 yrs	.0003	.0036	.0002		.0088	.0454	.0389	
5–10 yrs=10–15 yrs	.4282	.3937	.2380		.0360	.0297	.0022	
10–15 yrs=15–20 yrs	.0755	.0361	.0150		.7259	.8007	.5623	
15–20 yrs=20–30 yrs	.9513	.6290	.3249		.0123	.2431	.0426	
20–30 yrs=30 or more yrs	.6973	.9567	.7442		.4122	.0487	.2010	
5–10 yrs*education=0	.1928	.0036	.1138		.5435		.9151	
10–15 yrs*education=0	.1993	.2787	.5918		.7130		.1375	
15–20 yrs*education=0	.5440	.0333	.3303		.8130		.5427	
20–30 yrs*education=0	.0625	.2947	.9200		.0295		.0189	
30+ yrs*education=0	.4598	.4669	.4866		.8667		.6517	
All length of stay/education interactions=0	.3987		.6327	.5433	.3191		.1624	.2697
5–10 for < 12=5–10 for > 12				.5928				.4522
10–15 for < 12=10–15 for > 12				.5330				.3252
15–20 for < 12=15–20 for > 12				.7169				.4345
20–30 for < 12=20–30 for > 12				.0688				.6686
30+ yrs*education=0				.8562				.8716

P-Value

Table A.7

Full Regression by Country of Origin for Male Immigrants 25–60 Years Old in the United States (1970–1990)

Explanatory Variable	Mexico		United Kingdom, Canada		Europe		Japan, Korea, China	
	Coefficient	Std Err	Coefficient	Std Err	Coefficient	Std Err	Coefficient	Std Err
Immigrant	0.172	2.553	-7.572	3.948	2.883	2.770	4.279	4.545
In US 5-10 yrs	0.143	0.033	0.005	0.054	0.167	0.039	0.195	0.057
In US 10-15 yrs	0.157	0.038	0.104	0.048	0.176	0.035	0.285	0.066
In US 15-20 yrs	0.197	0.044	0.136	0.053	0.189	0.039	0.367	0.081
In US 20-30 yrs	0.163	0.063	0.239	0.061	0.187	0.045	0.433	0.116
In US 30+ yrs	0.208	0.092	0.288	0.078	0.172	0.059	0.669	0.169
Entered '85-'90	-0.317	0.061	0.227	0.061	-0.095	0.046	0.086	0.112
Entered '80-'84	-0.277	0.062	0.239	0.067	-0.025	0.049	-0.007	0.118
Entered '75-'79	-0.168	0.031	0.109	0.037	-0.025	0.026	0.036	0.059
Entered '70-'74	-0.083	0.035	0.078	0.046	-0.026	0.030	-0.015	0.069
Entered '60-'64	0.056	0.017	-0.050	0.028	0.053	0.020	0.028	0.034
Entered '50-'59	0.119	0.031	-0.127	0.032	0.038	0.023	-0.102	0.062
Entered before '50	0.115	0.057	-0.237	0.055	0.114	0.039	-0.158	0.109
1980 Census	2.277	0.503	2.572	0.505	2.545	0.502	2.449	0.507
1990 Census	-2.264	0.506	-2.424	0.508	-2.474	0.506	-2.504	0.510
Age	0.299	0.049	0.304	0.049	0.301	0.049	0.296	0.049
Age squared (i.e., Age2)	-0.870	0.183	-0.889	0.183	-0.878	0.183	-0.859	0.184
Age cubed (i.e., Age3)	0.117	0.030	0.120	0.030	0.119	0.030	0.116	0.030
Age to the fourth (i.e., Age4)	-0.063	0.018	-0.064	0.018	-0.063	0.018	-0.062	0.018
Immigrant*Age	-0.006	0.270	0.726	0.399	-0.325	0.280	-0.495	0.465
Immigrant*Age2	-0.174	1.055	-2.480	1.474	1.263	1.035	1.903	1.758
Immigrant*Age3	0.057	0.179	0.366	0.237	-0.210	0.167	-0.319	0.291
Immigrant*Age4	-0.050	0.112	-0.198	0.140	0.126	0.098	0.196	0.178
Age*1980	-0.259	0.051	-0.289	0.052	-0.287	0.051	-0.277	0.052
Age2*1980	1.002	0.192	1.114	0.192	1.104	0.191	1.068	0.193
Age3*1980	-0.162	0.031	-0.180	0.031	-0.179	0.031	-0.173	0.031
Age4*1980	0.095	0.018	0.106	0.018	0.105	0.018	0.102	0.018
Age*1990	0.231	0.052	0.248	0.052	0.253	0.052	0.256	0.052
Age2*1990	-0.964	0.193	-1.026	0.194	-1.045	0.193	-1.056	0.194
Age3*1990	0.173	0.031	0.183	0.031	0.186	0.031	0.188	0.031
Age4*1990	-0.112	0.019	-0.117	0.019	-0.119	0.019	-0.120	0.019
Immigrant*Age*1980	0.035	0.030	0.047	0.034	0.056	0.023	-0.076	0.055
Immigrant*Age2*1980	-0.149	0.222	-0.417	0.244	-0.417	0.164	0.644	0.403
Immigrant*Age3*1980	0.019	0.053	0.108	0.056	0.100	0.038	-0.163	0.096
Immigrant*Age4*1980	-0.005	0.040	-0.088	0.043	-0.077	0.028	0.127	0.074
Immigrant*Age*1990	0.008	0.030	0.010	0.035	0.048	0.024	-0.062	0.054
Immigrant*Age2*1990	0.076	0.214	-0.151	0.247	-0.292	0.171	0.488	0.392
Immigrant*Age3*1990	-0.034	0.051	0.044	0.057	0.061	0.039	-0.111	0.093
Immigrant*Age4*1990	0.033	0.039	-0.037	0.043	-0.042	0.030	0.078	0.071
Education 0-4	0.925	0.554	0.913	0.555	0.901	0.555	0.894	0.555
Education 5-8	1.280	0.554	1.268	0.555	1.256	0.555	1.250	0.555
Education 9	1.441	0.554	1.430	0.555	1.418	0.555	1.411	0.555
Education 10	1.491	0.554	1.479	0.555	1.467	0.555	1.461	0.555
Education 11	1.522	0.554	1.511	0.555	1.499	0.555	1.492	0.555
Education 13-15	-3.480	0.432	-3.460	0.433	-3.455	0.433	-3.454	0.433
Education 16	-3.246	0.432	-3.226	0.433	-3.221	0.433	-3.220	0.433
Education 17+	-3.160	0.432	-3.140	0.433	-3.135	0.433	-3.134	0.433
Immigrant*Educ 0-4	0.501	2.840	17.275	6.680	-5.697	3.911	-13.606	7.256
Immigrant*Educ 5-8	0.301	2.840	16.876	6.679	-6.003	3.911	-13.868	7.254
Immigrant*Educ 9	0.308	2.841	16.721	6.679	-6.135	3.911	-13.947	7.253
Immigrant*Educ 10	0.193	2.840	16.770	6.679	-6.161	3.911	-14.164	7.257
Immigrant*Educ 11	0.343	2.841	16.731	6.680	-6.133	3.911	-14.004	7.257
Immigrant*Educ 13-15	1.793	3.913	8.233	4.809	1.959	3.477	4.119	5.120
Immigrant*Educ 16	1.851	3.920	8.145	4.809	1.872	3.477	3.953	5.120
Immigrant*Educ 17+	2.116	3.913	8.153	4.809	1.920	3.477	3.984	5.120
1980*Educ 0-4	0.101	0.011	0.101	0.011	0.101	0.011	0.101	0.011
1980*Educ 5-8	0.002	0.005	0.002	0.005	0.002	0.005	0.002	0.005
1980*Educ 9	-0.037	0.007	-0.036	0.007	-0.036	0.007	-0.036	0.007
1980*Educ 10	-0.041	0.006	-0.041	0.006	-0.041	0.006	-0.041	0.006
1980*Educ 11	-0.031	0.007	-0.031	0.007	-0.031	0.007	-0.031	0.007
1980*Educ 13-15	-0.028	0.004	-0.028	0.004	-0.028	0.004	-0.028	0.004

Table A.7—continued

	(1) coef	(1) se	(2) coef	(2) se	(3) coef	(3) se	(4) coef	(4) se
1980*Educ 16	-0.071	0.005	-0.071	0.005	-0.071	0.005	-0.070	0.005
1980*Educ 17	-0.095	0.005	-0.095	0.005	-0.095	0.005	-0.095	0.005
1990*Educ 0-4	0.151	0.013	0.151	0.013	0.151	0.013	0.151	0.013
1990*Educ 5-8	-0.019	0.007	-0.018	0.007	-0.018	0.007	-0.018	0.007
1990*Educ 9	-0.091	0.008	-0.091	0.008	-0.091	0.008	-0.091	0.008
1990*Educ 10	-0.081	0.007	-0.081	0.007	-0.081	0.007	-0.081	0.007
1990*Educ 11	-0.070	0.007	-0.070	0.007	-0.070	0.007	-0.070	0.007
1990*Educ 13-15	0.039	0.004	0.039	0.004	0.039	0.004	0.039	0.004
1990*Educ 16	0.079	0.005	0.079	0.005	0.079	0.005	0.079	0.005
1990*Educ 17	0.207	0.005	0.207	0.005	0.207	0.005	0.207	0.005
Immigrant*1980*Educ 0-4	-0.090	0.051	-0.280	0.155	-0.160	0.046	-0.138	0.111
Immigrant*1980*Educ 5-8	-0.022	0.049	0.015	0.059	0.005	0.029	-0.087	0.093
Immigrant*1980*Educ 9	-0.113	0.077	0.107	0.083	0.011	0.056	-0.134	0.129
Immigrant*1980*Educ 10	0.020	0.082	0.065	0.065	0.027	0.048	0.248	0.171
Immigrant*1980*Educ 11	-0.146	0.096	0.229	0.073	-0.024	0.056	0.058	0.163
Immigrant*1980*Educ 13-15	0.074	0.077	0.034	0.044	0.010	0.033	-0.146	0.090
Immigrant*1980*Educ 16	-0.169	0.177	0.112	0.055	0.083	0.040	0.103	0.085
Immigrant*1980*Educ 17+	-0.393	0.119	0.153	0.048	0.103	0.034	0.039	0.074
Immigrant*1990*Educ 0-4	-0.067	0.050	-0.013	0.164	-0.148	0.050	-0.111	0.106
Immigrant*1990*Educ 5-8	0.023	0.047	0.161	0.079	0.058	0.034	-0.113	0.091
Immigrant*1990*Educ 9	-0.010	0.074	0.200	0.101	0.112	0.062	0.009	0.125
Immigrant*1990*Educ 10	0.047	0.079	0.166	0.081	0.125	0.055	0.064	0.168
Immigrant*1990*Educ 11	-0.108	0.094	0.180	0.087	-0.035	0.066	0.113	0.174
Immigrant*1990*Educ 13-15	0.067	0.074	0.045	0.042	-0.019	0.032	-0.165	0.087
Immigrant*1990*Educ 16	-0.143	0.173	0.105	0.053	0.009	0.039	0.005	0.082
Immigrant*1990*Educ 17+	-0.524	0.116	0.004	0.048	-0.045	0.034	-0.112	0.071
In US 5-10 yrs*Educ 0-11	-0.018	0.023	0.101	0.057	-0.020	0.039	0.060	0.045
In US 10-15 yrs*Educ 0-11	-0.012	0.024	0.152	0.056	0.048	0.036	0.080	0.054
In US 15-20 yrs*Educ 0-11	-0.054	0.025	0.157	0.053	0.055	0.035	0.124	0.059
In US 20-30 yrs*Educ 0-11	0.009	0.024	0.132	0.044	0.111	0.031	0.095	0.051
In US 30+ yrs*Educ 0-11	-0.058	0.031	0.060	0.042	0.063	0.033	0.047	0.049
In US 5-10 yrs*Educ 13+	-0.036	0.032	0.037	0.047	-0.082	0.036	0.014	0.034
In US 10-15 yrs*Educ 13+	0.021	0.032	0.006	0.045	-0.012	0.034	0.020	0.039
In US 15-20 yrs*Educ 13+	0.020	0.033	0.027	0.043	-0.008	0.033	0.062	0.045
In US 20-30 yrs*Educ 13+	0.055	0.027	-0.017	0.031	0.012	0.026	0.085	0.034
In US 30+ yrs*Educ 13+	0.054	0.033	0.005	0.032	0.013	0.027	0.038	0.038
Age*Educ 0-11	-0.147	0.056	-0.146	0.056	-0.144	0.056	-0.144	0.056
Age2*Educ 0-11	0.478	0.208	0.473	0.209	0.469	0.209	0.466	0.209
Age3*Educ 0-11	-0.068	0.034	-0.067	0.034	-0.067	0.034	-0.066	0.034
Age4*Educ 0-11	0.036	0.020	0.036	0.020	0.036	0.020	0.035	0.020
Age*Educ 13+	0.294	0.044	0.292	0.044	0.292	0.044	0.292	0.045
Age2*Educ 13+	-0.902	0.167	-0.893	0.167	-0.892	0.167	-0.891	0.167
Age3*Educ 13+	0.125	0.027	0.124	0.027	0.123	0.027	0.123	0.027
Age4*Educ 13+	-0.066	0.016	-0.065	0.016	-0.065	0.016	-0.065	0.016
Immigrant*Age*Educ 0-11	-0.041	0.298	-1.653	0.666	0.580	0.391	1.472	0.729
Immigrant*Age2*Educ 0-11	0.301	1.147	5.986	2.426	-1.933	1.431	-5.600	2.683
Immigrant*Age3*Educ 0-11	-0.074	0.191	-0.944	0.383	0.274	0.227	0.916	0.429
Immigrant*Age4*Educ 0-11	0.058	0.117	0.546	0.222	-0.140	0.132	-0.546	0.251
Immigrant*Age*Educ 13+	-0.146	0.412	-0.853	0.487	-0.250	0.351	-0.386	0.521
Immigrant*Age2*Educ 13+	0.419	1.590	3.164	1.800	1.100	1.294	1.322	1.942
Immigrant*Age3*Educ 13+	-0.056	0.266	-0.506	0.289	-0.203	0.207	-0.189	0.314
Immigrant*Age4*Educ 13+	0.030	0.163	0.295	0.170	0.134	0.122	0.096	0.187
Constant	2.427	0.479	2.377	0.480	2.407	0.478	2.455	0.481
Mean of Log Wages	6.278		6.298		6.298		6.296	
Number of Observations	1688217		1643500		1661731		1645859	
R-Squared	0.165		0.152		0.152		0.153	
F-test:								
Immig*Age=0 (DF=4)	2.38		1.86		1.92		1.16	
Educ*Age=0 and Immig*Educ*Age=0 (DF=16)	288.3*		289.4*		291.8*		296.1*	
Immig*Educ*Age=0 (DF=8)	6.92*		2.48		4.43*		3.09*	
Education*Age=0 (DF=8)	571.9*		570.7*		570.6*		569.4*	

NOTES: F-tests are differences in base year; interactions with census year dummies are not tested. DF=Degress of Freedom. F-tests include restrictions on all powers of age. *indicates significance at the .01 level. Parameter estimates for Age2, Age3, and Age4 multipled by 100, 1000, and 100,000, respectively.

Table A.7—continued

Explanatory Variable	Philippines Coefficient	Std Err	Middle East, Other Asia Coefficient	Std Err	Central America Coefficient	Std Err	Africa,Carib., S. Amer., Oc. Coefficient	Std Err
Immigrant	8.737	5.199	5.580	5.035	-1.469	5.088	0.250	3.152
In US 5-10 yrs	0.180	0.073	0.147	0.060	0.243	0.083	0.078	0.039
In US 10-15 yrs	0.088	0.095	0.154	0.089	0.128	0.119	0.221	0.061
In US 15-20 yrs	0.053	0.110	0.157	0.101	0.294	0.138	0.231	0.066
In US 20-30 yrs	0.067	0.174	0.392	0.163	0.234	0.223	0.304	0.111
In US 30+ yrs	-0.044	0.250	0.434	0.236	0.241	0.331	0.437	0.166
Entered '85-'90	-0.432	0.171	-0.137	0.159	-0.358	0.222	-0.014	0.110
Entered '80-'84	-0.392	0.177	-0.054	0.163	-0.436	0.226	0.013	0.112
Entered '75-'79	-0.141	0.088	-0.034	0.081	-0.158	0.114	-0.008	0.056
Entered '70-'74	-0.115	0.099	0.016	0.089	-0.239	0.125	0.072	0.060
Entered '60-'64	0.008	0.044	0.013	0.037	0.004	0.052	0.116	0.023
Entered '50-'59	0.192	0.089	-0.016	0.083	0.096	0.117	0.027	0.058
Entered before '50	0.373	0.166	-0.128	0.159	0.364	0.210	-0.012	0.112
1980 Census	2.503	0.506	2.485	0.507	2.472	0.507	2.528	0.505
1990 Census	-2.491	0.509	-2.532	0.510	-2.493	0.510	-2.454	0.508
Age	0.298	0.049	0.296	0.049	0.297	0.049	0.301	0.049
Age squared (i.e., Age2)	-0.869	0.183	-0.860	0.184	-0.864	0.184	-0.878	0.183
Age cubed (i.e., Age3)	0.117	0.030	0.116	0.030	0.116	0.030	0.119	0.030
Age to the fourth (i.e., Age4)	-0.063	0.018	-0.062	0.018	-0.062	0.018	-0.063	0.018
Immigrant*Age	-0.915	0.539	-0.466	0.520	0.150	0.540	-0.060	0.324
Immigrant*Age2	3.306	2.061	1.247	1.972	-0.683	2.143	0.276	1.228
Immigrant*Age3	-0.521	0.344	-0.122	0.326	0.123	0.373	-0.059	0.203
Immigrant*Age4	0.304	0.211	0.027	0.198	-0.080	0.240	0.044	0.123
Age*1980	-0.282	0.052	-0.281	0.052	-0.279	0.052	-0.285	0.052
Age2*1980	1.088	0.193	1.081	0.193	1.076	0.193	1.098	0.192
Age3*1980	-0.176	0.031	-0.175	0.031	-0.174	0.031	-0.178	0.031
Age4*1980	0.103	0.018	0.103	0.018	0.102	0.018	0.104	0.018
Age*1990	0.255	0.052	0.259	0.052	0.255	0.052	0.251	0.052
Age2*1990	-1.051	0.194	-1.067	0.194	-1.052	0.194	-1.037	0.194
Age3*1990	0.187	0.031	0.190	0.031	0.188	0.031	0.185	0.031
Age4*1990	-0.120	0.019	-0.121	0.019	-0.120	0.019	-0.118	0.019
Immigrant*Age*1980	0.038	0.067	-0.111	0.053	-0.064	0.092	0.002	0.034
Immigrant*Age2*1980	-0.158	0.489	0.836	0.391	0.546	0.684	-0.040	0.250
Immigrant*Age3*1980	0.026	0.115	-0.202	0.094	-0.140	0.166	0.014	0.059
Immigrant*Age4*1980	-0.016	0.088	0.157	0.073	0.114	0.129	-0.013	0.046
Immigrant*Age*1990	0.003	0.067	-0.081	0.052	0.032	0.090	0.015	0.035
Immigrant*Age2*1990	0.233	0.480	0.705	0.370	-0.108	0.654	-0.105	0.243
Immigrant*Age3*1990	-0.081	0.113	-0.186	0.088	0.016	0.157	0.026	0.057
Immigrant*Age4*1990	0.071	0.086	0.153	0.068	-0.009	0.123	-0.020	0.044
Education 0-4	0.898	0.554	0.893	0.555	0.896	0.554	0.903	0.555
Education 5-8	1.253	0.554	1.249	0.555	1.251	0.554	1.258	0.555
Education 9	1.414	0.554	1.410	0.555	1.412	0.554	1.419	0.555
Education 10	1.464	0.554	1.460	0.555	1.462	0.554	1.469	0.555
Education 11	1.496	0.554	1.491	0.555	1.493	0.554	1.501	0.555
Education 13-15	-3.454	0.432	-3.450	0.433	-3.454	0.433	-3.457	0.433
Education 16	-3.220	0.432	-3.216	0.433	-3.221	0.433	-3.224	0.433
Education 17+	-3.134	0.432	-3.131	0.433	-3.135	0.433	-3.138	0.433
Immigrant*Educ 0-4	-19.666	9.085	-17.220	8.310	6.257	6.302	-5.795	4.722
Immigrant*Educ 5-8	-19.828	9.088	-17.291	8.309	6.125	6.298	-6.069	4.722
Immigrant*Educ 9	-19.831	9.084	-17.556	8.314	6.199	6.302	-6.214	4.722
Immigrant*Educ 10	-20.045	9.086	-17.513	8.317	5.862	6.303	-6.189	4.722
Immigrant*Educ 11	-20.098	9.086	-17.411	8.303	5.643	6.299	-6.236	4.722
Immigrant*Educ 13-15	-7.438	5.916	-0.961	5.589	14.389	7.002	6.341	3.897
Immigrant*Educ 16	-7.473	5.916	-0.975	5.590	14.725	7.009	6.231	3.897
Immigrant*Educ 17+	-7.038	5.917	-1.015	5.590	14.330	7.006	6.310	3.897
1980*Educ 0-4	0.101	0.011	0.101	0.011	0.101	0.011	0.101	0.011
1980*Educ 5-8	0.002	0.005	0.002	0.005	0.002	0.005	0.002	0.005
1980*Educ 9	-0.036	0.007	-0.036	0.007	-0.036	0.007	-0.036	0.007
1980*Educ 10	-0.041	0.006	-0.041	0.006	-0.041	0.006	-0.041	0.006
1980*Educ 11	-0.031	0.007	-0.031	0.007	-0.031	0.007	-0.031	0.007
1980*Educ 13-15	-0.028	0.004	-0.028	0.004	-0.028	0.004	-0.028	0.004
1980*Educ 16	-0.070	0.005	-0.070	0.005	-0.071	0.005	-0.070	0.005

Table A.7—continued

1980*Educ 17	-0.095	0.005	-0.095	0.005	-0.095	0.005	-0.095	0.005
1990*Educ 0-4	0.151	0.013	0.151	0.013	0.151	0.013	0.151	0.013
1990*Educ 5-8	-0.018	0.007	-0.018	0.007	-0.018	0.007	-0.018	0.007
1990*Educ 9	-0.091	0.008	-0.091	0.008	-0.091	0.008	-0.091	0.008
1990*Educ 10	-0.081	0.007	-0.081	0.007	-0.081	0.007	-0.081	0.007
1990*Educ 11	-0.070	0.007	-0.070	0.007	-0.070	0.007	-0.070	0.007
1990*Educ 13-15	0.039	0.004	0.039	0.004	0.039	0.004	0.039	0.004
1990*Educ 16	0.079	0.005	0.079	0.005	0.079	0.005	0.079	0.005
1990*Educ 17	0.207	0.005	0.207	0.005	0.207	0.005	0.207	0.005
Immigrant*1980*Educ 0-4	-0.055	0.140	0.068	0.170	-0.156	0.230	-0.186	0.077
Immigrant*1980*Educ 5-8	-0.006	0.121	-0.019	0.118	-0.102	0.127	-0.036	0.047
Immigrant*1980*Educ 9	-0.115	0.193	0.317	0.217	-0.253	0.204	-0.005	0.085
Immigrant*1980*Educ 10	0.181	0.130	0.110	0.174	0.003	0.193	-0.086	0.081
Immigrant*1980*Educ 11	0.196	0.194	0.017	0.190	0.196	0.206	0.042	0.081
Immigrant*1980*Educ 13-15	0.174	0.092	0.012	0.083	0.120	0.125	0.005	0.048
Immigrant*1980*Educ 16	0.101	0.107	-0.023	0.088	-0.344	0.205	0.094	0.065
Immigrant*1980*Educ 17+	-0.108	0.097	0.177	0.073	0.120	0.171	0.162	0.052
Immigrant*1990*Educ 0-4	0.073	0.137	0.065	0.161	-0.106	0.223	-0.248	0.071
Immigrant*1990*Educ 5-8	-0.058	0.121	0.019	0.116	-0.138	0.122	-0.100	0.048
Immigrant*1990*Educ 9	0.085	0.203	0.115	0.209	-0.253	0.196	0.000	0.080
Immigrant*1990*Educ 10	0.170	0.140	0.160	0.165	-0.010	0.183	-0.108	0.079
Immigrant*1990*Educ 11	0.010	0.203	-0.145	0.192	0.208	0.199	-0.032	0.082
Immigrant*1990*Educ 13-15	0.134	0.088	0.008	0.079	0.035	0.119	0.001	0.046
Immigrant*1990*Educ 16	0.086	0.104	-0.063	0.083	-0.416	0.197	0.062	0.062
Immigrant*1990*Educ 17+	-0.255	0.097	0.072	0.070	-0.156	0.165	0.013	0.050
In US 5-10 yrs*Educ 0-11	0.091	0.062	0.084	0.052	0.050	0.039	0.020	0.034
In US 10-15 yrs*Educ 0-11	-0.009	0.066	0.252	0.059	0.060	0.046	0.014	0.038
In US 15-20 yrs*Educ 0-11	0.149	0.071	0.143	0.067	0.034	0.056	-0.010	0.040
In US 20-30 yrs*Educ 0-11	0.086	0.059	0.114	0.061	0.102	0.055	0.083	0.038
In US 30+ yrs*Educ 0-11	0.070	0.055	0.083	0.058	0.043	0.058	0.008	0.048
In US 5-10 yrs*Educ 13+	0.061	0.044	0.018	0.038	0.073	0.046	-0.003	0.030
In US 10-15 yrs*Educ 13+	0.077	0.045	0.138	0.042	0.028	0.053	0.048	0.033
In US 15-20 yrs*Educ13+	0.168	0.049	0.166	0.048	0.056	0.058	0.020	0.033
In US 20-30 yrs*Educ 13+	0.069	0.037	0.028	0.038	-0.004	0.040	0.067	0.028
In US 30+ yrs*Educ 13+	-0.010	0.042	0.052	0.043	0.030	0.044	0.017	0.037
Age*Educ 0-11	-0.144	0.056	-0.144	0.056	-0.144	0.056	-0.145	0.056
Age2*Educ 0-11	0.468	0.208	0.466	0.209	0.467	0.209	0.470	0.209
Age3*Educ 0-11	-0.066	0.034	-0.066	0.034	-0.066	0.034	-0.067	0.034
Age4*Educ 0-11	0.035	0.020	0.035	0.020	0.035	0.020	0.036	0.020
Age*Educ 13+	0.292	0.044	0.291	0.045	0.292	0.044	0.292	0.044
Age2*Educ 13+	-0.891	0.167	-0.890	0.167	-0.891	0.167	-0.893	0.167
Age3*Educ 13+	0.123	0.027	0.123	0.027	0.123	0.027	0.124	0.027
Age4*Educ 13+	-0.065	0.016	-0.065	0.016	-0.065	0.016	-0.065	0.016
Immigrant*Age*Educ 0-11	2.088	0.924	1.698	0.849	-0.622	0.662	0.632	0.480
Immigrant*Age2*Educ 0-11	-7.856	3.433	-5.946	3.171	2.435	2.548	-2.297	1.783
Immigrant*Age3*Educ 0-11	1.272	0.553	0.894	0.514	-0.413	0.425	0.361	0.288
Immigrant*Age4*Educ 0-11	-0.752	0.326	-0.492	0.305	0.255	0.260	-0.208	0.170
Immigrant*Age*Educ 13+	0.765	0.609	0.061	0.575	-1.490	0.733	-0.617	0.400
Immigrant*Age2*Educ 13+	-2.912	2.291	-0.150	2.166	5.671	2.807	2.173	1.502
Immigrant*Age3*Educ 13+	0.477	0.374	0.015	0.354	-0.945	0.467	-0.333	0.245
Immigrant*Age4*Educ 13+	-0.285	0.224	-0.007	0.212	0.580	0.284	0.188	0.146
Constant	2.430	0.480	2.453	0.481	2.442	0.480	2.406	0.480
Mean of Log Wages	6.296		6.297		6.294		6.294	
Number of Observations	1639681		1643401		1638288		1651879	
R-Squared	0.152		0.153		0.155		0.153	
F-test:*								
Immig*Age=0 (DF=4)	1.15		1.91		1.74		7.24*	
Educ*Age=0 and	287.5*		288.8*		286.3*		288.3*	
Immig*Educ*Age=0 (DF=16)								
Immig*Educ*Age=0 (DF=8)	1.77		3.76*		1.76		2.51*	
Education*Age=0 (DF=8)	571.8*		569.6*		571.1*		570.2*	

NOTES: F-tests are differences in base year; interactions with census year dummies are not tested. DF=Degress of Freedom. F-tests include restrictions on all powers of age. *indicates significance at the .01 level. Parameter estimates for Age2, Age3, and Age4 multiplied by 100, 1000, and 100,000, respectively.

Table A.8

Full Regression by Country of Origin for Male Immigrants 25–60 Years Old in California (1970–1990)

Explanatory Variable	Mexico Coefficient	Std Err	United Kingdom, Canada Coefficient	Std Err	Europe Coefficient	Std Err	Japan, Korea, China Coefficient	Std Err
Immigrant	0.956	2.834	-5.574	5.776	2.065	4.571	5.385	5.309
In US 5-10 yrs	0.169	0.037	-0.009	0.078	0.172	0.064	0.248	0.070
In US 10-15 yrs	0.178	0.044	0.173	0.073	0.194	0.060	0.395	0.080
In US 15-20 yrs	0.224	0.051	0.203	0.079	0.150	0.067	0.456	0.098
In US 20-30 yrs	0.178	0.074	0.317	0.094	0.223	0.082	0.573	0.139
In US 30+ yrs	0.206	0.109	0.481	0.124	0.220	0.110	0.819	0.203
Entered '85-'90	-0.341	0.071	0.355	0.093	-0.050	0.081	0.224	0.134
Entered '80-'84	-0.300	0.072	0.316	0.100	0.077	0.084	0.108	0.141
Entered '75-'79	-0.189	0.037	0.105	0.054	-0.029	0.045	0.091	0.070
Entered '70-'74	-0.107	0.040	0.099	0.067	-0.005	0.052	0.054	0.082
Entered '60-'64	0.048	0.018	-0.064	0.037	0.090	0.031	0.034	0.040
Entered '50-'59	0.126	0.037	-0.165	0.048	0.029	0.040	-0.175	0.074
Entered before '50	0.151	0.067	-0.323	0.082	0.105	0.070	-0.257	0.129
1980 Census	4.085	1.062	4.717	1.079	4.834	1.076	4.423	1.085
1990 Census	-2.927	1.065	-3.436	1.085	-3.368	1.082	-3.657	1.090
Age	0.498	0.109	0.506	0.110	0.514	0.110	0.484	0.110
Age squared (i.e., Age2)	-1.574	0.406	-1.602	0.411	-1.632	0.410	-1.519	0.412
Age cubed (i.e., Age3)	0.226	0.066	0.231	0.067	0.236	0.066	0.218	0.067
Age to the fourth (i.e., Age4)	-0.125	0.039	-0.128	0.040	-0.130	0.039	-0.120	0.040
Immigrant*Age	-0.071	0.300	0.566	0.583	-0.272	0.463	-0.563	0.544
Immigrant*Age2	0.000	1.175	-2.008	2.159	1.158	1.720	2.039	2.069
Immigrant*Age3	0.038	0.200	0.305	0.348	-0.203	0.278	-0.331	0.346
Immigrant*Age4	-0.043	0.126	-0.169	0.206	0.124	0.166	0.199	0.213
Age*1980	-0.448	0.109	-0.513	0.110	-0.525	0.110	-0.483	0.111
Age2*1980	1.699	0.405	1.939	0.412	1.983	0.411	1.828	0.414
Age3*1980	-0.272	0.066	-0.311	0.067	-0.318	0.067	-0.293	0.067
Age4*1980	0.158	0.039	0.181	0.040	0.185	0.039	0.171	0.040
Age*1990	0.306	0.109	0.358	0.111	0.351	0.111	0.380	0.111
Age2*1990	-1.244	0.407	-1.440	0.415	-1.414	0.413	-1.523	0.416
Age3*1990	0.219	0.066	0.250	0.067	0.246	0.067	0.264	0.067
Age4*1990	-0.138	0.039	-0.157	0.040	-0.154	0.040	-0.165	0.040
Immigrant*Age*1980	0.046	0.037	0.068	0.054	0.089	0.044	-0.113	0.078
Immigrant*Age2*1980	-0.205	0.269	-0.566	0.386	-0.644	0.316	0.845	0.564
Immigrant*Age3*1980	0.030	0.064	0.140	0.090	0.149	0.073	-0.197	0.133
Immigrant*Age4*1980	-0.013	0.049	-0.109	0.068	-0.111	0.055	0.146	0.101
Immigrant*Age*1990	0.010	0.036	-0.007	0.054	0.089	0.045	-0.124	0.077
Immigrant*Age2*1990	0.047	0.262	-0.078	0.389	-0.644	0.319	0.815	0.552
Immigrant*Age3*1990	-0.024	0.062	0.031	0.090	0.148	0.074	-0.173	0.130
Immigrant*Age4*1990	0.024	0.048	-0.027	0.068	-0.108	0.056	0.118	0.099
Education 0-4	1.010	1.185	0.942	1.192	0.950	1.194	0.914	1.194
Education 5-8	1.261	1.185	1.194	1.194	1.202	1.194	1.165	1.194
Education 9	1.371	1.185	1.304	1.192	1.312	1.194	1.275	1.194
Education 10	1.403	1.185	1.336	1.192	1.344	1.194	1.307	1.194
Education 11	1.434	1.185	1.367	1.192	1.375	1.194	1.338	1.194
Education 13-15	-1.658	0.785	-1.570	0.789	-1.570	0.791	-1.559	0.791
Education 16	-1.454	0.785	-1.366	0.789	-1.367	0.790	-1.356	0.791
Education 17+	-1.352	0.785	-1.263	0.789	-1.264	0.791	-1.253	0.791
Immigrant*Educ 0-4	1.842	3.259	12.941	11.141	-2.347	7.074	-15.577	8.765
Immigrant*Educ 5-8	1.711	3.259	12.926	11.149	-2.611	7.071	-15.720	8.761
Immigrant*Educ 9	1.808	3.260	12.662	11.151	-2.651	7.072	-15.686	8.759
Immigrant*Educ 10	1.711	3.260	12.709	11.152	-2.653	7.071	-15.958	8.766
Immigrant*Educ 11	1.834	3.261	12.572	11.152	-2.659	7.071	-15.740	8.766
Immigrant*Educ 13-15	0.268	4.343	3.575	6.828	-2.506	5.515	2.608	5.995
Immigrant*Educ 16	0.329	4.351	3.374	6.828	-2.658	5.516	2.461	5.995
Immigrant*Educ 17+	0.586	4.346	3.565	6.829	-2.573	5.515	2.435	5.996
1980*Educ 0-4	0.128	0.028	0.130	0.028	0.129	0.028	0.129	0.028
1980*Educ 5-8	-0.024	0.013	-0.023	0.013	-0.023	0.013	-0.023	0.013
1980*Educ 9	-0.035	0.017	-0.034	0.017	-0.034	0.017	-0.034	0.017
1980*Educ 10	-0.042	0.015	-0.042	0.015	-0.042	0.015	-0.042	0.015
1980*Educ 11	-0.027	0.014	-0.027	0.014	-0.027	0.014	-0.027	0.014
1980*Educ 13-15	-0.012	0.009	-0.012	0.009	-0.012	0.009	-0.012	0.009

Table A.8—continued

1980*Educ 16	-0.029	0.011	-0.029	0.011	-0.029	0.011	-0.029	0.011
1980*Educ 17	-0.072	0.010	-0.072	0.010	-0.072	0.010	-0.071	0.010
1990*Educ 0-4	0.077	0.031	0.079	0.031	0.078	0.031	0.078	0.031
1990*Educ 5-8	-0.074	0.017	-0.074	0.018	-0.074	0.018	-0.073	0.018
1990*Educ 9	-0.077	0.021	-0.077	0.021	-0.077	0.021	-0.077	0.021
1990*Educ 10	-0.097	0.016	-0.097	0.016	-0.097	0.016	-0.097	0.016
1990*Educ 11	-0.079	0.015	-0.079	0.015	-0.078	0.015	-0.078	0.015
1990*Educ 13-15	0.036	0.008	0.036	0.008	0.036	0.008	0.037	0.008
1990*Educ 16	0.094	0.011	0.094	0.011	0.094	0.011	0.095	0.011
1990*Educ 17	0.216	0.011	0.215	0.011	0.215	0.011	0.216	0.011
Immigrant*1980*Educ 0-4	-0.161	0.067	0.054	0.330	-0.172	0.101	-0.201	0.145
Immigrant*1980*Educ 5-8	-0.014	0.060	0.116	0.108	0.092	0.061	-0.098	0.117
Immigrant*1980*Educ 9	-0.179	0.094	0.202	0.133	-0.034	0.111	-0.216	0.160
Immigrant*1980*Educ 10	-0.042	0.100	0.104	0.102	0.121	0.098	0.290	0.233
Immigrant*1980*Educ 11	-0.170	0.111	0.395	0.107	0.027	0.110	-0.075	0.196
Immigrant*1980*Educ 13-15	0.004	0.095	0.086	0.066	0.014	0.058	-0.219	0.110
Immigrant*1980*Educ 16	-0.263	0.213	0.239	0.086	0.130	0.070	0.030	0.113
Immigrant*1980*Educ 17+	-0.475	0.169	0.135	0.075	0.086	0.063	0.024	0.104
Immigrant*1990*Educ 0-4	-0.044	0.066	0.191	0.308	-0.154	0.105	-0.044	0.140
Immigrant*1990*Educ 5-8	0.063	0.060	-0.234	0.154	0.171	0.069	-0.035	0.115
Immigrant*1990*Educ 9	-0.077	0.091	0.220	0.178	0.043	0.120	-0.033	0.157
Immigrant*1990*Educ 10	0.003	0.097	0.259	0.126	0.135	0.103	0.059	0.229
Immigrant*1990*Educ 11	-0.117	0.109	0.504	0.132	-0.024	0.127	0.024	0.207
Immigrant*1990*Educ 13-15	0.013	0.092	0.065	0.064	0.040	0.057	-0.165	0.106
Immigrant*1990*Educ 16	-0.196	0.208	0.235	0.084	0.097	0.069	-0.007	0.110
Immigrant*1990*Educ 17+	-0.589	0.166	-0.067	0.075	0.017	0.063	-0.037	0.100
In US 5-10 yrs*Educ 0-11	-0.042	0.026	0.066	0.090	-0.021	0.066	0.010	0.056
In US 10-15 yrs*Educ 0-11	-0.041	0.027	0.001	0.090	0.047	0.063	0.059	0.069
In US 15-20 yrs*Educ 0-11	-0.078	0.028	0.093	0.087	0.016	0.063	0.110	0.079
In US 20-30 yrs*Educ 0-11	-0.026	0.028	0.033	0.070	0.044	0.054	0.073	0.067
In US 30+ yrs*Educ 0-11	-0.081	0.040	-0.093	0.074	0.034	0.061	0.014	0.073
In US 5-10 yrs*Educ 13+	-0.030	0.036	0.070	0.066	-0.119	0.056	-0.030	0.041
In US 10-15 yrs*Educ 13+	0.030	0.037	0.078	0.064	0.050	0.053	-0.031	0.048
In US 15-20 yrs*Educ 13+	0.023	0.038	0.086	0.060	0.068	0.052	0.033	0.055
In US 20-30 yrs*Educ 13+	0.083	0.034	0.034	0.045	0.043	0.041	0.085	0.045
In US 30+ yrs*Educ 13+	0.116	0.044	0.020	0.049	0.050	0.046	0.116	0.054
Age*Educ 0-11	-0.132	0.120	-0.125	0.121	-0.125	0.121	-0.122	0.121
Age2*Educ 0-11	0.407	0.447	0.380	0.450	0.383	0.450	0.369	0.451
Age3*Educ 0-11	-0.054	0.072	-0.050	0.072	-0.050	0.072	-0.048	0.073
Age4*Educ 0-11	0.027	0.042	0.025	0.043	0.025	0.043	0.024	0.043
Age*Educ 13+	0.111	0.081	0.101	0.081	0.101	0.081	0.100	0.081
Age2*Educ 13+	-0.223	0.303	-0.187	0.305	-0.188	0.305	-0.183	0.305
Age3*Educ 13+	0.015	0.049	0.009	0.050	0.009	0.050	0.009	0.050
Age4*Educ 13+	-0.001	0.029	0.003	0.030	0.003	0.030	0.003	0.030
Immigrant*Age*Educ 0-11	-0.206	0.342	-1.321	1.108	0.222	0.709	1.630	0.878
Immigrant*Age2*Educ 0-11	0.975	1.309	4.992	4.026	-0.616	2.595	-6.083	3.221
Immigrant*Age3*Educ 0-11	-0.193	0.218	-0.812	0.635	0.066	0.412	0.979	0.513
Immigrant*Age4*Educ 0-11	0.134	0.132	0.481	0.367	-0.021	0.240	-0.576	0.300
Immigrant*Age*Educ 13+	0.010	0.458	-0.425	0.690	0.203	0.557	-0.209	0.610
Immigrant*Age2*Educ 13+	-0.142	1.766	1.709	2.551	-0.571	2.055	0.624	2.270
Immigrant*Age3*Educ 13+	0.032	0.295	-0.291	0.409	0.061	0.329	-0.074	0.367
Immigrant*Age4*Educ 13+	-0.021	0.181	0.179	0.240	-0.017	0.193	0.027	0.218
Constant	0.388	1.063	0.314	1.075	0.234	1.073	0.534	1.079
Mean of Log Wages	6.349		6.409		6.408		6.404	
Number of Observations	558365		514944		520204		520045	
R-Squared	0.188		0.142		0.142		0.145	
F-test:*								
Immig*Age=0 (DF=4)	2.68*		1.62		2.98*		2.95*	
Educ*Age=0 and Immig*Educ*Age=0 (DF=16)	62.98*		62.33*		62.03*		62.7*	
Immig*Educ*Age=0 (DF=8)	5.06*		0.75		1.07		1.77	
Education*Age=0 (DF=8)	123.3*		122*		121.6*		121.6*	

NOTES: F-tests are differences in base year; interactions with census year dummies are not tested. DF=Degress of Freedom. F-tests include restrictions on all powers of age. *indicates significance at the .01 level. Parameter estimates for Age2, Age3, and Age4 multipled by 100, 1000, and 100,000, respectively.

Table A.8—continued

Explanatory Variable	Philippines Coefficient	Std Err	Middle East, Other Asia Coefficient	Std Err	Central America Coefficient	Std Err	Africa,Carib., S. Amer.,Oc. Coefficient	Std Err
Immigrant	13.287	5.814	5.992	6.153	4.596	5.910	9.832	5.410
In US 5-10 yrs	0.198	0.087	0.127	0.080	0.282	0.100	0.065	0.068
In US 10-15 yrs	0.102	0.115	0.078	0.124	0.269	0.148	0.420	0.104
In US 15-20 yrs	0.100	0.134	0.127	0.140	0.470	0.172	0.331	0.113
In US 20-30 yrs	0.091	0.213	0.416	0.232	0.485	0.283	0.531	0.190
In US 30+ yrs	-0.033	0.311	0.298	0.337	0.584	0.420	0.784	0.285
Entered '85-'90	-0.400	0.210	-0.152	0.227	-0.132	0.280	0.222	0.189
Entered '80-'84	-0.374	0.216	-0.079	0.231	-0.214	0.284	0.325	0.191
Entered '75-'79	-0.105	0.107	-0.025	0.115	-0.060	0.143	0.091	0.096
Entered '70-'74	-0.099	0.120	0.036	0.126	-0.152	0.155	0.219	0.103
Entered '60-'64	-0.006	0.049	0.032	0.049	0.010	0.060	0.128	0.037
Entered '50-'59	0.179	0.110	-0.023	0.119	0.001	0.147	-0.090	0.099
Entered before '50	0.361	0.206	-0.024	0.221	0.196	0.255	-0.154	0.182
1980 Census	4.635	1.081	4.724	1.086	4.548	1.084	4.743	1.083
1990 Census	-3.474	1.087	-3.544	1.091	-3.505	1.090	-3.461	1.089
Age	0.501	0.110	0.502	0.110	0.496	0.110	0.506	0.110
Age squared (i.e., Age2)	-1.583	0.411	-1.587	0.413	-1.563	0.412	-1.603	0.412
Age cubed (i.e., Age3)	0.228	0.067	0.228	0.067	0.225	0.067	0.231	0.067
Age to the fourth (i.e., Age4)	-0.126	0.040	-0.126	0.040	-0.124	0.040	-0.128	0.040
Immigrant*Age	-1.387	0.602	-0.528	0.636	-0.429	0.631	-1.043	0.562
Immigrant*Age2	5.090	2.315	1.595	2.429	1.302	2.544	4.020	2.163
Immigrant*Age3	-0.816	0.390	-0.204	0.406	-0.176	0.453	-0.688	0.364
Immigrant*Age4	0.483	0.241	0.094	0.250	0.089	0.297	0.436	0.226
Age*1980	-0.504	0.110	-0.513	0.111	-0.495	0.111	-0.515	0.111
Age2*1980	1.908	0.413	1.942	0.414	1.875	0.414	1.949	0.413
Age3*1980	-0.306	0.067	-0.311	0.067	-0.301	0.067	-0.313	0.067
Age4*1980	0.178	0.040	0.181	0.040	0.175	0.040	0.182	0.040
Age*1990	0.362	0.111	0.369	0.112	0.365	0.111	0.360	0.111
Age2*1990	-1.454	0.415	-1.481	0.417	-1.466	0.416	-1.449	0.416
Age3*1990	0.252	0.067	0.257	0.068	0.254	0.067	0.252	0.067
Age4*1990	-0.158	0.040	-0.161	0.040	-0.159	0.040	-0.158	0.040
Immigrant*Age*1980	0.058	0.091	-0.056	0.082	-0.113	0.127	-0.040	0.072
Immigrant*Age2*1980	-0.304	0.659	0.386	0.607	0.938	0.953	0.183	0.527
Immigrant*Age3*1980	0.061	0.155	-0.085	0.146	-0.240	0.232	-0.021	0.127
Immigrant*Age4*1980	-0.046	0.117	0.058	0.113	0.193	0.182	-0.001	0.099
Immigrant*Age*1990	0.025	0.091	-0.044	0.081	-0.047	0.127	-0.061	0.072
Immigrant*Age2*1990	0.038	0.648	0.371	0.583	0.414	0.932	0.255	0.521
Immigrant*Age3*1990	-0.031	0.151	-0.095	0.139	-0.105	0.226	-0.028	0.125
Immigrant*Age4*1990	0.031	0.115	0.076	0.108	0.082	0.177	0.001	0.097
Education 0-4	0.934	1.189	0.931	1.194	0.929	1.191	0.938	1.193
Education 5-8	1.185	1.189	1.183	1.194	1.181	1.191	1.189	1.193
Education 9	1.295	1.189	1.293	1.194	1.291	1.191	1.300	1.193
Education 10	1.327	1.189	1.325	1.194	1.323	1.191	1.332	1.193
Education 11	1.358	1.189	1.356	1.194	1.354	1.191	1.363	1.193
Education 13-15	-1.569	0.787	-1.556	0.791	-1.570	0.788	-1.565	0.790
Education 16	-1.366	0.787	-1.352	0.791	-1.366	0.788	-1.361	0.790
Education 17+	-1.263	0.787	-1.250	0.791	-1.264	0.788	-1.259	0.790
Immigrant*Educ 0-4	-20.778	10.484	-14.444	10.342	2.233	7.272	-9.375	8.860
Immigrant*Educ 5-8	-20.858	10.488	-14.406	10.341	2.202	7.268	-9.597	8.858
Immigrant*Educ 9	-20.856	10.486	-14.520	10.347	2.362	7.271	-9.552	8.856
Immigrant*Educ 10	-21.008	10.481	-14.187	10.343	2.193	7.271	-9.750	8.860
Immigrant*Educ 11	-21.175	10.490	-14.408	10.337	1.703	7.268	-9.638	8.859
Immigrant*Educ 13-15	-14.050	6.619	-1.558	6.903	9.342	8.077	-2.371	6.432
Immigrant*Educ 16	-14.240	6.619	-1.492	6.903	9.827	8.084	-2.464	6.433
Immigrant*Educ 17+	-13.869	6.619	-1.667	6.903	9.285	8.080	-2.424	6.432
1980*Educ 0-4	0.129	0.028	0.130	0.028	0.129	0.028	0.130	0.028
1980*Educ 5-8	-0.024	0.013	-0.023	0.013	-0.023	0.013	-0.023	0.013
1980*Educ 9	-0.035	0.017	-0.034	0.017	-0.034	0.017	-0.034	0.017
1980*Educ 10	-0.042	0.015	-0.042	0.015	-0.042	0.015	-0.042	0.015
1980*Educ 11	-0.028	0.014	-0.027	0.014	-0.027	0.014	-0.027	0.014
1980*Educ 13-15	-0.012	0.009	-0.012	0.009	-0.012	0.009	-0.012	0.009
1980*Educ 16	-0.029	0.011	-0.029	0.011	-0.029	0.011	-0.029	0.011

Table A.8—continued

1980*Educ 17	-0.071	0.010	-0.071	0.010	-0.071	0.010	-0.072	0.010
1990*Educ 0-4	0.078	0.031	0.079	0.031	0.078	0.031	0.079	0.031
1990*Educ 5-8	-0.074	0.018	-0.074	0.018	-0.074	0.018	-0.073	0.018
1990*Educ 9	-0.077	0.021	-0.077	0.021	-0.077	0.021	-0.077	0.021
1990*Educ 10	-0.097	0.016	-0.097	0.016	-0.097	0.016	-0.097	0.016
1990*Educ 11	-0.079	0.015	-0.079	0.015	-0.079	0.015	-0.078	0.015
1990*Educ 13-15	0.037	0.008	0.037	0.008	0.037	0.008	0.036	0.008
1990*Educ 16	0.095	0.011	0.094	0.011	0.094	0.011	0.094	0.011
1990*Educ 17	0.216	0.011	0.216	0.011	0.215	0.011	0.215	0.011
Immigrant*1980*Educ 0-4	-0.168	0.200	0.233	0.314	-0.229	0.296	-0.266	0.177
Immigrant*1980*Educ 5-8	-0.031	0.153	0.146	0.179	-0.127	0.171	-0.045	0.103
Immigrant*1980*Educ 9	-0.061	0.224	0.312	0.360	-0.356	0.238	-0.173	0.173
Immigrant*1980*Educ 10	0.177	0.179	-0.223	0.314	-0.268	0.246	0.087	0.166
Immigrant*1980*Educ 11	0.300	0.233	0.112	0.266	0.153	0.297	-0.070	0.169
Immigrant*1980*Educ 13-15	0.086	0.115	0.054	0.117	0.070	0.163	-0.037	0.088
Immigrant*1980*Educ 16	0.156	0.142	-0.062	0.131	-0.529	0.297	0.031	0.123
Immigrant*1980*Educ 17+	-0.073	0.145	0.241	0.115	0.047	0.239	0.093	0.104
Immigrant*1990*Educ 0-4	0.109	0.190	0.172	0.307	-0.093	0.289	-0.328	0.163
Immigrant*1990*Educ 5-8	0.005	0.154	0.079	0.177	-0.141	0.166	-0.107	0.105
Immigrant*1990*Educ 9	-0.077	0.244	0.017	0.346	-0.343	0.230	-0.280	0.171
Immigrant*1990*Educ 10	0.221	0.186	-0.112	0.307	-0.250	0.235	-0.042	0.166
Immigrant*1990*Educ 11	0.125	0.248	-0.144	0.265	0.259	0.290	-0.179	0.178
Immigrant*1990*Educ 13-15	0.096	0.111	0.041	0.112	0.020	0.157	0.032	0.085
Immigrant*1990*Educ 16	0.221	0.139	-0.086	0.126	-0.572	0.288	0.084	0.118
Immigrant*1990*Educ 17+	-0.147	0.145	0.165	0.111	-0.136	0.234	0.051	0.102
In US 5-10 yrs*Educ 0-11	0.000	0.079	0.077	0.069	-0.002	0.046	0.036	0.063
In US 10-15 yrs*Educ 0-11	-0.109	0.086	0.342	0.078	0.018	0.055	-0.014	0.070
In US 15-20 yrs*Educ 0-11	0.000	0.096	0.087	0.097	-0.017	0.070	0.110	0.073
In US 20-30 yrs*Educ 0-11	-0.079	0.079	0.042	0.088	0.040	0.071	0.212	0.068
In US 30+ yrs*Educ 0-11	-0.098	0.087	-0.057	0.102	-0.100	0.094	-0.072	0.089
In US 5-10 yrs*Educ 13+	0.064	0.051	0.027	0.049	0.093	0.055	-0.037	0.050
In US 10-15 yrs*Educ 13+	0.066	0.053	0.174	0.054	0.074	0.064	0.007	0.053
In US 15-20 yrs*Educ13+	0.154	0.059	0.155	0.061	0.100	0.071	0.029	0.053
In US 20-30 yrs*Educ 13+	0.080	0.048	-0.041	0.054	0.017	0.055	0.041	0.046
In US 30+ yrs*Educ 13+	0.065	0.061	0.197	0.067	0.126	0.068	0.042	0.060
Age*Educ 0-11	-0.124	0.121	-0.123	0.121	-0.123	0.121	-0.124	0.121
Age2*Educ 0-11	0.377	0.449	0.375	0.451	0.375	0.449	0.378	0.450
Age3*Educ 0-11	-0.049	0.072	-0.049	0.073	-0.049	0.072	-0.050	0.072
Age4*Educ 0-11	0.024	0.043	0.024	0.043	0.024	0.043	0.024	0.043
Age*Educ 13+	0.101	0.081	0.100	0.081	0.101	0.081	0.101	0.081
Age2*Educ 13+	-0.187	0.304	-0.182	0.305	-0.187	0.304	-0.186	0.305
Age3*Educ 13+	0.009	0.049	0.008	0.050	0.009	0.050	0.009	0.050
Age4*Educ 13+	0.003	0.029	0.003	0.030	0.003	0.030	0.003	0.030
Immigrant*Age*Educ 0-11	2.147	1.068	1.392	1.057	-0.216	0.765	0.994	0.901
Immigrant*Age2*Educ 0-11	-7.939	3.970	-4.848	3.947	0.855	2.944	-3.697	3.354
Immigrant*Age3*Educ 0-11	1.269	0.640	0.725	0.639	-0.140	0.492	0.600	0.542
Immigrant*Age4*Educ 0-11	-0.743	0.378	-0.398	0.379	0.081	0.301	-0.359	0.321
Immigrant*Age*Educ 13+	1.433	0.680	0.129	0.709	-0.964	0.846	0.286	0.662
Immigrant*Age2*Educ 13+	-5.354	2.555	-0.425	2.665	3.632	3.242	-1.215	2.496
Immigrant*Age3*Educ 13+	0.865	0.416	0.064	0.434	-0.597	0.539	0.216	0.408
Immigrant*Age4*Educ 13+	-0.511	0.249	-0.039	0.259	0.362	0.328	-0.138	0.244
Constant	0.366	1.075	0.353	1.080	0.416	1.078	0.313	1.078
Mean of Log Wages	6.402		6.406		6.396		6.404	
Number of Observations	516255		516522		515025		515851	
R-Squared	0.145		0.143		0.153		0.144	
F-test:*								
Immig*Age=0 (DF=4)	1.86		0.83		1.17		4.73*	
Educ*Age=0 and	62.5*		62.6*		61.6*		61.6*	
Immig*Educ*Age=0 (DF=16)								
Immig*Educ*Age=0 (DF=8)	1.59		2.17		1.11		1.24	
Education*Age=0 (DF=8)	122.6*		121.6*		122.3*		121.8*	

NOTES: F-tests are differences in base year; interactions with census year dummies are not tested. DF=Degress of Freedom. F-tests include restrictions on all powers of age. *indicates significance at the .01 level. Parameter estimates for Age2, Age3, and Age4 multiplied by 100, 1000, and 100,000, respectively.

REFERENCES

Ahmed, Bashir, and J. Gregory Robinson (1994). "Estimates of Emigration of the Foreign-Born Population: 1980–1990," *Population Estimates and Projections Technical Working Paper #9*, Washington, D.C.: Population Division, Bureau of the Census, December.

Baker, Michael, and Dwayne Benjamin (1994). "The Performance of Immigrants in the Canadian Labor Market," *Journal of Labor Economics*, 12(3): 369–405.

Borjas, George J. (1995). "Assimilation and Changes in Cohort Quality Revisited: What Happened to Immigrant Earnings in the 1980s?" *Journal of Labor Economics*, 13(2): 201–245.

Borjas, George J. (1994). "The Economics of Immigration," *Journal of Economic Literature*, XXXII(4):1667–1717.

Borjas, George J. (1993). "Immigration Policy, National Origin, and Immigrant Skills: A Comparison of Canada and the United States," David Card and Richard B. Freeman, eds., *Small Differences That Matter: Labor Markets and Income Maintenance in Canada and the United States*, Chicago, Ill.: University of Chicago Press, pp. 21–43.

Borjas, George J. (1990). *Friends or Strangers: The Impact of Immigrants on the U.S. Economy*, New York: Basic Books.

Borjas, George J. (1989). "Immigrant and Emigrant Earnings: A Longitudinal Study," *Economic Inquiry*, XXVII(January): 21–37.

Borjas, George J. (1987). "Self-Selection and the Earnings of Immigrants," *American Economic Review*, 77(4): 531–553.

Borjas, George J. (1985). "Assimilation, Changes in Cohort Quality, and the Earnings of Immigrants," *Journal of Labor Economics*, 3(4): 463–489.

Borjas, George J. (1982). "The Earnings of Male Hispanic Immigrants in the United States," *Industrial and Labor Relations Review*, 35(3): 343–353.

Borjas, George J., and Brent Bratsberg (1994). "Who Leaves? The Outmigration of the Foreign-Born," mimeo, San Diego, Calif.: University of California, San Diego, August.

Borjas, George J., and Marta Tienda (1989). "The Employment and Wages of Legalized Immigrants," *International Migration Review*, XXVII(4): 712–747.

Bound, John, and Timothy Waidmann (1992). "Disability Transfers, Self-Reported Health, and the Labor Force Participation of Older Men: Evidence from the Historical Record," *Quarterly Journal of Economics* 107: 1393–1419.

Carliner, Geoffrey (1980). "Wages, Earnings, and Hours of First, Second, and Third Generation American Males," *Economic Inquiry*, 18(1): 87–102.

Chiswick, Barry R. (1986). "Human Capital and the Labor Market Adjustment of Immigrants: Testing Alternative Hypotheses," Oded Stark, ed., *Research in Human Capital Development*, JAI Press Inc.

Chiswick, Barry R. (1978). "The Effect of Assimilation on the Earnings of Foreign-Born Men," *Journal of Political Economy*, 86(5): 897–921.

Duleep, Harriet Orcutt, and Mark C. Regets, eds. (1992). "The Elusive Concept of Immigrant Quality," mimeo, Washington, D.C.: Urban Institute.

Fernandez, Edward W., and J. Gregory Robinson (1994). "Illustrative Ranges of the Distribution of Undocumented Immigrants by

State," *Population Estimates and Projections Technical Working Paper #8,* Washington, D.C.: Population Division, Bureau of the Census, October.

Friedberg, Rachel M. (1991). "The Labor Market Assimilation of Immigrants in the United States: The Role of Age at Arrival," mimeo, Cambridge, Mass.: Massachusetts Institute of Technology, December.

Funkhauser, Edward (1995a). "How Much of Immigration Assimilation Is Related to English Language Acquisition?" mimeo, Santa Barbara, Calif.: Department of Economics, University of California, Santa Barbara.

Funkhauser, Edward (1995b). "The Negative Relationship Between Labor Market Outcomes and English Language Ability: Is It Who You Are, Where You Live, or Who You Live With?" mimeo, Santa Barbara, Calif.: Department of Economics, University of California, Santa Barbara.

Funkhauser, Edward, and Stephen J. Trejo (1995). "The Labor Market Skills of Recent Male Immigrants: Evidence from the Current Population Survey," *Industrial and Labor Relations Review,* 48(4): 792–811.

Garvey, Deborah L. (1995). "Immigrants' Earnings and Labor Market Assimilation: A Case Study of New Jersey," mimeo, Princeton, N.J.: Princeton University Department of Economics, March.

Greenwood, Michael J. (1986). "The Factor Market Consequences of U.S. Immigration," *Journal of Economic Literature,* 24(4): 1738–1772.

Greenwood, Michael J., and John M. McDowell (1990). "The Labor Market Consequences of U.S. Immigration: A Survey," Washington, D.C.: U.S. Department of Labor, Bureau of International Labor Affairs.

Grenier, Gilles (1984). "The Effects of Language Characteristics on the Wages of Hispanic-American Males," *Journal of Human Resources,* 19(1): 35–52.

Jasso, Guillermina, and Mark R. Rosenzweig (1982). "Estimating the Emigration Rates of Legal Immigrants Using Administrative and Survey Data: The 1971 Cohort of Immigrants to the United States," *Demography*, 19(3): 279–290.

Kossoudji, Sherrie A. (1988). "Immigrant Worker Assimilation: Is It a Labor Market Phenomenon?" *Journal of Human Resources*, XXIV(3): 494–527.

LaLonde, Robert J., and Robert H. Topel (1992). "The Assimilation of Immigrants in the U.S. Labor Market," George J. Borjas and Richard B. Freeman, eds., *Immigration and the Work Force*, Chicago, Ill.: The University of Chicago Press.

Long, James E. (1980). "The Effect of Americanization on Earnings," *Journal of Political Economy*, 88(3): 620–629.

McManus, Walter, William Gould, and Finis Welch (1983). "Earnings of Hispanic Men: The Role of English Language Proficiency," *Journal of Labor Economics*, 1(2): 101–130.

Murphy, Kevin, and Finis Welch (1990). "Empirical Age–Earnings Profiles," *Journal of Labor Economics*, 8 (April): 202–229.

Park, Jin Heum (1994). "Changes in U.S. School Quality: What Do We Learn from Immigrants?" mimeo, Princeton, N.J.: Department of Economics, Princeton University.

Parsons, Donald (1980). "The Decline in Male Labor Force Participation," *Journal of Political Economy*, 88(1): 117–134.

Reimers, Cordelia W. (1995). "The Progress of Mexican Immigrants in U.S. Labor Markets, 1980 to 1990," mimeo, New York, N.Y.: Hunter College.

Smith, James P. (unpublished). "Hispanics and the American Dream: An Analysis of Hispanic Male Labor Market Wages, 1940–1980," RAND research, mimeo.

Stewart, James B., and Thomas Hyclak (1984). "An Analysis of the Earnings Profiles of Immigrants," *Review of Economics and Statistics*, 66(2): 292–296.

Tienda, Marta, and Audrey Singer (1995). "Wage Mobility of Undocumented Workers in the United States," *International Migration Review*, XXIX(1): 112–138.

Warren, Robert, and Jennifer Marks Peck (1980). "Foreign-Born Emigration from the United States: 1960–1970," *Demography*, 17(1): 71–84.

Yuengart, A. M. (1994). "Immigrant Earnings, Relative to What? Importance of Earnings Function Specification and Comparison Points," *Journal of Applied Econometrics*, 9: 71–90.